Sir John Betjeman in 1974, at the gate of his
childhood home, 31 West Hill, Highgate, London.

Deeply I loved thee, 31 West Hill!
At that hill's foot did London then begin . . .

SUMMONED BY BELLS

Portrait by Derek Hill 1979

John Betjeman

A LIFE IN PICTURES

Compiled and introduced by Bevis Hillier

JOHN MURRAY
in association with The Herbert Press

This selection © John Murray 1984
Editorial text © Bevis Hillier 1984

First published 1984 by
John Murray (Publishers) Ltd
50 Albemarle Street, London W1X 4BD
in association with The Herbert Press Ltd
46 Northchurch Road, London N1 4EJ

Printed in Great Britain by
Jolly & Barber Ltd, Rugby
Bound in Great Britain by
The Pitman Press, Bath

British Library Cataloguing in Publication Data

ISBN 0-7195-4181-6

Contents

Preface

A journalist friend of mine was reminded by his editor that one picture is worth a thousand words. 'Not a thousand of *my* words!' was the haughty reply.

I hope that this book will be regarded as a complement to the full biography of Sir John Betjeman which I am now writing, not as a 'soft option' for it; though I have not scrupled to plunder that biography for captions to photographs – taking advantage of the slightly archaic literary convention by which cuttings from the text are grafted on to illustrations. ('"Look!" said Amanda, "It's the tramp again!"')

In 1976 Sir John agreed that I should be his biographer. Since nearly all my earlier books had been on art or the decorative arts, it was natural for me to set as much store by pictures as by words. John Betjeman lent me many photographs; and wherever I went in my quest for memories of his life, I searched through family albums, often obtaining permission to borrow them and make copies.

There were some unexpected pictorial coups. Pierce Synnott, whose mansion at Naas, County Kildare, was the first 'stately home' John stayed in, sadly died before he could talk to me about his undergraduate memories of John, as he had agreed to do; but he sent a registered packet of John's letters, and with them were photographs of John at the age of twenty, of Synnott in plus-fours, Patrick Balfour (later Lord Kinross) in a kilt and Balfour's mother, of whom John was fond. When I stayed with Frances, Lady Fergusson of Kilkerran, near Ayr in Scotland to talk about her brother, John's friend the late Michael Dugdale, she produced Dugdale's photograph albums. One of them contained a picture of 'Colonel' Kolkhorst, John's eccentric friend among the Oxford dons, holding a doll. Before that, the only portrait of Kolkhorst I knew was Osbert Lancaster's caricature in the second volume of his autobiography, *With an Eye to the Future* (1967). Most of the pictures in this book have never been reproduced before.

On the simplest level – taken literally at its *face* value – this distillation of family albums is a visual record of John Betjeman's life. But it is more than that. When pictures are brought into relationship with each other (even if no more subtly than by a stamp-collector's making up of 'sets') new resonances are created: the aggregate is more valuable than the sum of the individual elements. Proust wrote that every man over forty is responsible for his face, and that idea was also the theme of Wilde's *Portrait of Dorian Gray*. But what stays the same in a face can be as revealing as that which changes. In the long sequence of images of John, the luminous, wounded eyes last from the baby pictures to those of old age. They suggest guilt, curiosity, tenderness and a continuing puzzlement at the world's follies, unimpaired by the resources of satire he could train on them. John's friend Kingsley Amis has observed how the accusing glare of adolescence replaces the wide-eyed gaze of childhood. In the case of John, who cheerfully cast himself as a classic example of arrested development, the transition was never made. He remained the wide-eyed boy who always knew when the emperor was wearing no clothes.

But the pictures are not just a visual archive of Betjeman's life. They are also a gallery of the society and literary/artistic circles of his times. Eliot, Auden, Waugh, Anthony Powell are here, with some less famous who deserve to be remembered, such as Martyn Skinner, who won the Hawthornden Prize in 1941 with his poem *Letters to Malaya*. He was John's exact contemporary at Magdalen College, Oxford; one of John's poems is dedicated to him; and John helped to get published Skinner's admired epic, *The Return of Arthur* (1966) and his elegiac poem *Old Rectory* (in three parts, 1970, 1973 and 1977).

In the Introduction to Betjeman's *Uncollected Poems* in 1982, I wrote: 'Betjeman's poetry . . . petrifies for ever a particular brief period in time – what for want of a better word might be called the

"Art Deco" period, the time of Betjeman's youth . . .' Some of the pictures collected here do this visually, as John's poems do it verbally. They represent the same slice of social history – admittedly a slice with more icing-sugar than most. It is the world of *Brideshead Revisited*, of Powell's *Dance to the Music of Time*. Only vestiges of it remain today, like the small bone at the base of the spine which indicated to Darwin that man once had a tail.

In his precocious autobiography *Lions and Shadows*, Christopher Isherwood (whose Berlin stories were adapted by John van Druten into a play called *I Am A Camera*) tells how he hit on the idea of breaking up his narrative into self-contained scenes – 'an epic in an album of snapshots'. In the same passage he describes what it is that a book of this kind can give one – something that can never be conveyed by a written biography, in which 'there are wearisome interrelationships to be disentangled and explained, or you have got to plough through the hero's childhood, which is almost certain to be a bore'. The first snapshot might be a group of men and women drinking cocktails in nearly modern dress, the fashions of the year before last; the second, an Edwardian tea-party. 'What

charming, funny costumes! But hullo – wait a minute! We seem to recognize some of the figures. That young girl in the enormous hat; surely she's the small Eton-cropped woman of forty with the well-preserved figure? Yes, she is!' In a third snapshot, immediately post-war, one can see what ten years have done to these men and women. 'Some of them have disappeared altogether from the earlier scene: and that little boy in the foreground has nearly grown up.' The final snapshot, of the present day, looks at first sight identical with the first –

But . . . if you look at these faces more closely, there is all the difference in the world. It is the difference made by knowledge. In the first snapshot, we saw these people merely as casual acquaintances: here they are our intimate friends. With the eyes of friends, we look deeply into their faces, reading, in Time's cipher, everything which is secretly written there. And this sends us back to the first snapshot. With how much more interest we examine it now! Every attitude, every gesture, seems charged with meaning, with reference to things past, with presage of things to come. And so we go through our album once again. And again and again and again. There is no reason, theoretically, why you should ever stop reading this kind of book at all.

Origins

John Betjeman was born at 52 Parliament Hill Mansions, south of Highgate, London, on 28 August 1906.

His mother sent beribboned cards to her friends.

Parliament Hill Mansions (still standing) is a terracotta-coloured block of Victorian flats.

That early flat, electrically lit,
Red silk and leather in the dining-room,
Beads round the drawing-room electrolier...
Singing in bed, to make the youngster laugh,
Tosti's 'Goodbye', Lord Henry's 'Echo Song' –
And windy walks on Sunday to the Heath,
While dogs were barking round the White Stone Pond ...

SUMMONED BY BELLS

John's father was Ernest Betjemann (1872–1934). A sporty, outdoor man, he despised John for his ineptitude at shooting.

'How many times must I explain
The way a boy should hold a gun?'
I recollect my father's pain
At such a milksop for a son.

HERTFORDSHIRE

John himself was born Betjemann – with two 'n's. But when the First World War broke out, a German-sounding name became a disadvantage: John was taunted as a 'German spy' at school. By his late teens he was using an earlier form of the family name, with only one 'n'.

John's mother was Mabel Bessie Betjemann (1878–1952). When John was nine, she made some pin-money by running a millinery and dress business in Buckingham Street, London, under the alias of 'Mrs Betty Burton'.

I feared my father, loved my mother more,
And just because of this would criticize,
In my own mind, the artless things she said.
 'Dr Macmillan, who's so good and cheap,
Says I will tire my kidneys if I stoop,
And oh, I do love gardening, for now
My garden is the last thing I have left.
You'll help me with the weeding, won't you, John?'

SUMMONED BY BELLS

THE SATURDAY SALON.

Millinery. Blouses, etc.

OPEN on SATURDAY AFTERNOONS ONLY
from 1.30 to 5.30.

19 BUCKINGHAM STREET,
STRAND, W.C.
(Two minutes from Charing Cross).

Under the direction of Mrs. BETTY BURTON.

✗ Denotes position of Saturday Salon.

THE SATURDAY SALON has been inaugurated to meet a long-felt need on the part of women engaged in war work or other business, who owing to the earlier closing of the west-end shops, are experiencing great difficulty in finding the time in which to purchase suitable and well-cut wearing apparel. I am therefore starting this little venture at the suggestion of several friends engaged in business, who, like hundreds of other women similarly placed, are utterly weary of the unsatisfactory method of shopping ten minutes before closing time, or in a rush during the luncheon hour. My motto may be summed up in the words "No Need to Hurry."

John's mother told him that the Betjeman family was Dutch in origin, and had come to England in the late eighteenth century. But it is more likely that the family was originally German, from the area known as *Die Heide* (The Heath) near Bremen in Lower Saxony. Some of his ancestors were in the sugar-refining trade.

The family does seem to have arrived in London in the late eighteenth century. John's great-grandfather, George Betjeman, a maker of patent dressing cases in Clerkenwell, London, spelt his surname with one 'n'; later, with the fashion for all things German in the Victorian period, the name was altered to 'Betjemann'.

John's father, who vainly hoped he would join him in the firm as the fourth generation,

showed me old George Betjeman's book . . .
'December eighteen seven. Twelve and six –
For helping brother William with his desk.'
Uninteresting then it seemed to me,
Uninteresting still.

Summoned by Bells

Drawn by Tho. H. Shepherd.

ST. LEONARD'S, SHOREDITCH.

In the eighteenth and early nineteenth centuries, many of the Betjeman/Betjemann family lived in the East End of London, a traditional habitat for European immigrants. St George's in the East and St Leonard's Shoreditch were among the churches where they were baptized, married and buried.

St Botolph Bishopsgate was another church patronized by immigrants, including the Dutch tea-seller Augustus Teetgen who founded his firm (now defunct) nearby in 1834 and issued a tin caddy (opposite) depicting the church. John's grandfather was a churchwarden there.

When the great bell
BOOMS over the Portland stone urn, and
From the carved cedar wood
Rises the odour of incense,
I SIT DOWN
In St Botolph Bishopsgate Churchyard
And wait for the spirit of my grandfather
Toddling along from the Barbican.

City

The Betjeman and Merrick families were doubly linked: not only did Rebecca Betjeman marry John Merrick in 1846; her brother, John's great-grandfather George, married John Merrick's sister Mary-Anne. John Merrick's father William, who like George Betjeman was a cabinet-maker in Clerkenwell, was alleged to belong to the ancient Meyrick family of Bodorgan, Anglesey, which claimed descent from a Welsh prince. This fifteenth-century stained-glass window in Llangadwaladr church, Anglesey, shows Owen ap Meurig in full field armour of the Wars of the Roses period.

The family and the business moved to north London. John's parents were married in St Saviour's, Aberdeen Park, Highbury, on which he wrote a poem.

A great Victorian church, tall, unbroken and bright
In a sun that's setting in Willesden
*   and saturating us here.*
These were the streets my parents knew
*   when they loved and won . . .*

These were the streets they knew;
*   and I, by descent, belong*
To these tall neglected houses divided into flats.
Only the church remains, where carriages
*   used to throng*
And my mother stepped out in flounces
*   and my father stepped out in spats*
To shadowy stained-glass matins or gas-lit evensong
And back in a country quiet with
*   doffing of chimney hats.*

Great red church of my parents,
*   cruciform crossing they knew –*
Over these same encaustics
*   they and their parents trod*
Bound through a red-brick transept
*   for a once familiar pew*

Where the organ set them singing
and the sermon let them nod
And up this coloured brickwork
the same long shadows grew
As these in the stencilled chancel
where I kneel in the presence of God . . .

Sadly, the church is now closed and boarded up.

John's immediate ancestors were small-time tradespeople. His grandfather, John Betjemann, who served an apprenticeship in cabinet-making and entered the family dressing-case business, married in 1870 Hannah Thompson (below), daughter of Edward John Thompson, a watch material maker and his wife Jessie (*née* Roberts). His father Ernest, who also joined the family firm, married in 1902 Mabel Bessie Dawson, daughter of James Dawson, a manufacturer of artificial flowers, and his wife Alice Jane (*née* Daniel).

The firm of G. Betjemann & Sons had become prosperous through the patenting, by John's grandfather, of the Tantalus, a sort of cage in which wine and spirit decanters could be locked to stop the servants helping themselves to the contents. John claimed his grandfather, John Betjemann, had died from sampling too much of the decanters' contents.

. . . And those decanters which had brought us down
And Islington and Highbury and larks
And sprees at Collinses' when I could hear,
Laugh with Dan Leno, join in Colbourn's song,
'The Man Who Broke the Bank . . .'
and mount again
The knife board omnibus and hear the wheels
Go silent over straw in Upper Street.
Jack Spuling, Tommy Godfrey, oyster bars,
Returning squiffy in the family brougham
And William's 'Master Ernest, something's up!
They've left the gas on full inside the 'all.'
And there was father dead upstairs at last
And the decanters shining on the side.

From 'The Epic', an early version of SUMMONED BY BELLS: the passage was omitted from the published work.

TANTALUS SPIRIT STANDS.

The "B" quality Tantalus.

Well finished in oak, walnut, or mahogany.
English cut bottles.
Nickel bar, &c.
Bramah lock.

DESCRIPTION.		THREE BOTTLES. No.	Each.	TWO BOTTLES. No.	Each.
Polished Oak, Walnut, or Mahogany, fitted full cut quart bottles	...	T297	£6 4 0	T298	£4 16 0
" " " " half cut		T299	5 16 0	T300	4 10 0
" " " " plain		T301	5 4 0	T302	4 2 0
" " " " full cut pint		T303	4 17 0	T304	3 12 0
" " " " half cut		T305	4 13 0	T306	3 16 0
" " " " plain		T307	4 4 0	T308	3 10 0

The "C" quality.

Solid oak and nickel.
English cut bottles.
Good finish.

DESCRIPTION.		THREE BOTTLES. No.	Each.	TWO BOTTLES. No.	Each.
Polished Oak, fitted full cut quart bottles	...	T309	£5 8 0	T310	£4 8 0
" " " " half cut		T311	5 0 0	T312	4 4 6
" " " " plain		T313	4 14 0	T314	4 0 0
" " " " full cut pint		T315	4 4 0	T316	3 8 0
" " " " half cut		T317	4 0 0	T318	3 4 6
" " " " plain		T319	3 17 0	T320	3 0 0

The "D" quality.
Solid oak and nickel.
Cut glass bottles.

DESCRIPTION.		THREE BOTTLES. No.	Each.	TWO BOTTLES. No.	Each.
Polished Oak, fitted full cut quart bottles	...	T321	£5 0 0	T322	£4 0 0
" " " " half cut		T323	4 17 0	T324	3 18 0
" " " " plain		T325	4 14 0	T326	3 16 0
" " " " full cut pint		T327	3 16 0	T328	3 2 0
" " " " half cut		T329	3 14 0	T330	3 0 6
" " " " plain		T331	3 12 0	T332	2 19 0

G. B. & S.   LONDON.

The showroom of G. Betjemann & Sons, Pentonville Road, in the 1920s.

> *When you rang*
> *The front-door bell a watchful packer pulled*
> *A polished lever twenty yards away,*
> *And this released the catch into a world*
> *Of shining showrooms full of secret drawers*
> *And Maharajahs' dressing-cases . . .*
> *Why now*
> *When, staying in a quiet country house,*
> *I see an onyx ashtray of the firm,*
> *Or in my bedroom, find the figured wood*
> *Of my smooth-sliding dressing-table drawers*
> *Has got a look about it of the Works,*
> *Does my mind flinch so?*

SUMMONED BY BELLS

By the 1920s, elaborate dressing-tables were an important part of Betjemann's manufacture. Many of them were sold by Asprey of New Bond Street, London. (John and Eric Asprey were close friends of Ernest Betjemann, who used to go on shoots with them, occasionally accompanied by John.)

John sometimes went on the firm's annual outing – to Southend, Hastings, Margate or Wormley by the River Lea. Ernest Betjemann would travel down in his car with the managing director Horace Andrew; the men in solid-tyre Daimler charabancs from the Carrimore Motor Service. Lunch was held in a big restaurant, with speeches by Ernest Betjemann and by Andrew. One of Ernest's workmen, Bill Hammond, recalled: 'John took his father's place at one of our outings to Southend. He stood up to make a speech and apologised for the fact that he'd got one brown shoe and one black; and he added "I have to tell you that I have another pair at home exactly the same."' After lunch, Betjemann and Andrew would leave the men to their high jinks.

Near Essex of the River Lea
  And anglers out with hook and worm
And Epping Forest glades where we
  Had beanfeasts with my father's firm.

At huge and convoluted pubs
  They used to set us down from brakes
In that half-land of football clubs
  Which London near the Forest makes.

ESSEX

14

Highgate

'An only child, deliciously alone . . .'

When John was still a baby, his parents moved to 31 West Hill, Highgate – higher in the social graph than Parliament Hill Mansions. The photograph of 1909 shows No.31 to the right, and No.30 to the left, with the next-door neighbour, Ethelwynne Bouman, holding her daughter Betty. Both houses are still standing, though some damage was caused to No.31 in 1976 by an arsonist's attack.

At that hill's foot did London then begin,
With yellow horse-trams clopping past the planes
To grey-brick nonconformist Chetwynd Road
And on to Kentish Town and barking dogs
And costers' carts and crowded grocers' shops
And Daniels' store, the local Selfridge's,
The Bon Marché, the Electric Palace, slums
That thrilled me with their smells of poverty –
Till, safe once more, we gained the leafy slope
And buttered toast and 31 West Hill.

SUMMONED BY BELLS

The horse-drawn trams remained a nostalgic memory for John; but West Hill was also the terminus of the electric tramcar services numbered 7 to 15. Exciting shopping expeditions began outside Charrington, Sells, Dale & Co., coal merchants, on the west side of the Kentish Town Road, where samples of coal were displayed in miniature railway wagons. Kentish Town was the poor neighbour of Highgate. In his poem 'Parliament Hill Fields' John remembered riding in a tram past Zwanziger the baker's (of which the windows were broken by vicious anti-Germans during the First World War, when John was taunted about his own surname).

When the Bon Marché was shuttered,
> *when the feet were hot and tired,*
Outside Charrington's we waited,
> *by the 'STOP HERE IF REQUIRED',*
Rocked past Zwanziger the baker's,
> *and the terrace blackish brown,*
And the curious Anglo-Norman parish church
> *of Kentish Town.*

John aged four, in his Sunday best.

John with his mother: a studio photograph taken in Kentish Town Road. The date has been cut off, but was probably 1910.

The Betjemanns' next-door neighbours on West Hill were what the Betjemanns thought they themselves were: Dutch. Never naturalized, Jan Bouman, a journalist, was born and died a Dutchman. His wife Ethelwynne was of Scottish and Cumbrian parentage. They had three children – Bill (born 1907), Mary (born 1908) and Betty (born 1909). Bill, one year younger than John, was his great friend and companion, a handsome and lovable child, though a severe attack of scarlet fever had, in his sister Mary's words, 'left something missing'. John regarded the Boumans as his second family, and was desolated when they moved to Holland in 1916; though Mary Bouman only realized that years later, when she and her sister had a reunion lunch with him in the Betjeman room of the Charing Cross Hotel, London, in September 1979 (centre, above).

> *I could also tell*
> *That we were slightly richer than my friends,*
> *The family next door: we owned a brougham*
> *And they would envy us our holidays.*

SUMMONED BY BELLS

Even as a small child, John showed the dramatic talent which was later to be so evident in his television performances.

As an only child with few friends, John made a
confidant and friend of his teddy-bear Archibald,
who survived into patched old age. Evelyn Waugh
pirated him for Lord Sebastian's bear in *Brideshead
Revisited*; and John made him the hero of a children's
story, *Archie and the Strict Baptists*, published in
1977 with illustrations by Phillida Gili based on his
sketches.

> *. . . Archibald, my safe old bear,*
> *Whose woollen eyes looked sad or glad at me,*
> *Whose ample forehead I could wet with tears,*
> *Whose half-moon ears received my confidence,*
> *Who made me laugh, who never let me down.*
> *I used to wait for hours to see him move,*
> *Convinced that he could breathe. One dreadful day*
> *They hid him from me as a punishment:*
> *Sometimes the desolation of that loss*
> *Comes back to me and I must go upstairs*
> *To see him in the sawdust, so to speak,*
> *Safe and returned to his idolator.*

SUMMONED BY BELLS

John's first school was Byron House, Highgate, a
Montessori establishment founded in 1895. The
photograph below shows him on the left. One of his
contemporaries there was Philip Harben, later well
known as 'the television cook'.

Along the Grove, what happy, happy steps
Under the limes I took to Byron House,
And blob-work, weaving, carpentry and art . . .

    SUMMONED BY BELLS

At Byron House John met his first love, Peggy
Purey-Cust, the daughter of Admiral Sir Herbert
Purey-Cust of 82 West Hill.

O Peggy Purey-Cust, how pure you were:
My first and purest love, Miss Purey-Cust!
Satchel on back I hurried up West Hill
To catch you on your morning walk to school,
Your nanny with you and your golden hair
Streaming like sunlight. Strict deportment made
You hold yourself erect and every step
Bounced up and down as though you walked on springs.
Your ice-blue eyes, your lashes long and light,
Your sweetly freckled face and turned-up nose
So haunted me that all my loves since then
Have had a look of Peggy Purey-Cust . . . .

    SUMMONED BY BELLS

John was less happy at Highgate Junior School, which he attended after Byron House. There were bullies among both masters and boys. But one master who did not bully him was T. S. Eliot, known as 'the American master'. Eliot, who had previously taught at High Wycombe Grammar School, taught the upper forms of Highgate Junior for the three terms of 1916. The two poets became friends in the 1930s, when Eliot reminded Betjeman that John had presented him with a manuscript called *The Best of Betjeman*.

That dear good man, with Prufrock in his head
And Sweeney waiting to be agonized,
I wonder what he thought? He never says
When now we meet, across the port and cheese.
He looks the same as then, long, lean and pale,
Still with the slow deliberating speech
And enigmatic answers. At the time
A boy called Jelly said: 'He thinks they're bad' –
But he himself is still too kind to say.

Summoned by Bells

Hopeless Dawn by Frank Bramley (Tate Gallery, London)

Once when my father took me to the Tate
We stood enraptured by 'The Hopeless Dawn',
The picture first to move me. Twenty times,
They told me, had Frank Bramley watched the flame
Expiring in its candlestick before
He put it down on canvas. Guttering there,
It symbolized the young wife's dying hope
And the old mother's – gazing out to sea:
The meal upon the table lay prepared
But no good man to eat it: through the panes,
An angry sea below the early light

Tossed merciless, as I had seen the waves
In splendid thunder over Greenaway
Send driftwood shooting up the beach as though
Great planks were light as paper. 'Put it down!
Translate the picture into verse, my boy,
And here's your opening–

  Through the humble cottage window
    Streams the early dawn.'

SUMMONED BY BELLS

The Dragon School

Dragon School, Oxford –
The Carpenter's Shop.

From 1917 to 1920, John was a boarder at the Dragon School, Oxford – also known as 'Lynam's' and 'the O.P.S.' (Oxford Preparatory School). One of his masters there, 'Bruno' Brown, recalls him as 'a sensitive and far from typical Prep School boy, and little, if at all, interested in games of any sort. However not many boys of 13 went about with a volume of Charles Dibdin's poems – the author of *Tom Bowling* – in their pockets, or had already become fascinated with architecture – both foretastes of things to come.'

In the playground was the carpentry shop. If a boy was naughty or idle, 'Bruno' Brown would send him to the woodwork master for 'something to beat you with'. (The boy was likely to return bearing a twelve-foot plank and grinning widely.)

The Dragon School was run by two brothers,
C.C. Lynam ('Skipper'), and A.E. Lynam ('Hum', so
called because he hummed while doing the rounds of
the dormitories to give the boys the chance of *not*
being caught out of bed).

Before the hymn the Skipper would announce
The latest names of those who'd lost their lives
For King and Country and the Dragon School.
Sometimes his gruff old voice was full of tears
When a particular favourite had been killed.
Then we would hear the nickname of the boy,
'Pongo' or 'Podge', and how he'd played 3Q
For Oxford and, if only he had lived,
He might have played for England – which he did,
But in a grimmer game against the Hun.
And then we'd all look solemn, knowing well
There'd be no extra holiday today.

    SUMMONED BY BELLS

yours ever
Skipper

In the group photograph here, John is on the left between the master's knees.

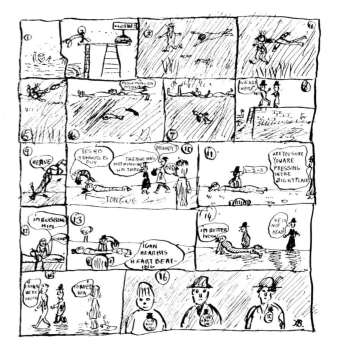

The school magazine, *The Draconian* (the cover had been designed by Leonard Campbell Taylor, an Old Draconian, in 1900) published the boys' ages, weights and heights at the beginning of each term. At the beginning of Christmas Term, 1918, John was 12.3 years old and weighed 4 stone 11 lb and 4 oz. (an increase of 4 oz. over the previous term) and was 4ft 7½in. tall. Hugh Gaitskell, the future Labour Leader, was in the same list.

John's earliest published poems and prose pieces appeared in *The Draconian*.

Cartoon by John in *The Draconian* of September 1920, 'One Answer to Question 9'. (Question 9 of the General Paper was: Explain fully and illustrate with drawings how you would rescue and revive a drowning person.')

IN MEMORIAM, A.E.L., M.A.L.

Hum and May went out one day
  On a motor-bike painted vermillion;
Hum was the nut of the latest cut
  And May was the girl on the pillion.

J. BETJEMANN.

Whatever will rhyme with the Summer?
There only is ' plumber ' and ' drummer ':
Why! the cleverest bard
Would find it quite hard
To concoct with the Summer,—a plumber!

My mind's getting glummer and glummer.
Hooray! *there's* a word besides drummer;
Oh, I *will* think of some
Ere the prep's end has come,
But the rimes will get rummer and rummer.

Ah!—If the bee hums, it's a hummer;
And the bee showeth signs of the Summer;
Also holiday babels
Make th' porter gum labels,
And whenever he gums, he's a gummer!

The cuckoo's a goer and comer,
He goes in the hot days of Summer;
But he cucks ev'ry day
Till you plead and you pray
That his voice will get dumber and dumber!

J. BETJEMANN, age 13. 6

In 1918 John took the part of Ruth in the Dragon School production of Gilbert and Sullivan's *The Pirates of Penzance*. Reviewing it in the school magazine, R.E.C.W. wrote: 'A pleasing buxom wench was Ruth who scored a great success in the part of "Maid of all work". Always perfectly self-possessed she enunciated her lines with a clearness which even in that company was remarkable.'

The cast also included the future Sir Percival Mallalieu (the 'Percy Mandeville' who figures in *Summoned by Bells* – 'the perfect boy . . . Upright and honourable, good at games' – who challenged John to a fight from which John escaped by claiming 'My mater's very ill.') Hugh Gaitskell was in the Chorus of Police.

In 1920 John took two parts in the Dragon School production of *Henry V*: the Earl of Cambridge and Charles VI, King of France. Gabriel Carritt, later a great friend of W.H. Auden, was also in the cast, which again included Percy Mallalieu.

In the photograph below, John is in the middle of the second row from the front (with a shield behind him) wearing the costume of the King of France.

Reviewing the play, Frank Sidgwick wrote of F. Wylie's Henry:

'It was a gallant performance, and I don't think anyone else could have been cast for the part. Except, perhaps, Betjemann. Having beheld him manufacture, out of two small parts, the Earl of Cambridge and the King of France, two separate, distinct and perfect gems of character-acting, I am not prepared to say that he could not have acted, with equal insight and genius, Henry the Fifth, Fourth, Sixth or Eighth, or Othello, Falstaff, Imogen, Caliban, Hamlet, Juliet's Nurse, Ariel or Lance *and* his dog Crab. I can't give higher praise than by saying that he ought to play Bottom; but if next year he is cast for the part of Biondello in the *Taming of the Shrew*, who I believe has little to do except eat an apple, I will again break all engagements to come and see him do it.'

Cornwall

The Betjemanns spent their summer holidays at Trebetherick, north Cornwall.

The holidays began with the long train ride from London to Wadebridge.

> *. . . the long express from Waterloo*
> *That takes us down to Cornwall. Tea-time shows*
> *The small fields waiting, every blackthorn hedge*
> *Straining inland before the south-west gale.*
> *The emptying train, wind in the ventilators,*
> *Puffs out of Egloskerry to Tresméer*
> *Through minty meadows, under bearded trees*
> *And hills upon whose sides the clinging farms*
> *Hold Bible Christians. Can it really be*
> *That this same carriage came from Waterloo?*
> *On Wadebridge station what a breath of sea*
> *Scented the Camel valley! Cornish air,*
> *Soft Cornish rains, and silence after steam . . .*

SUMMONED BY BELLS

Map of the Wadebridge, Padstow, Tintagel and Boscastle District.
On the scale of two miles to the inch.

LONDON & SOUTH-WESTERN RAILWAY.

Cheap Tickets to the West Country

FROM LONDON (WATERLOO STATION), Etc.
. . . as under . . .

TOURIST TICKETS (all classes)
Available for 6 months, are issued to all the principal places during the Summer, and to certain resorts during the Winter. These Tickets allow break of journey *en route.* Also

CIRCULAR-TOUR TICKETS (RAIL & COACH)
Embracing all the beauty spots and quaint old-world places in North Devon and North Cornwall, and including Coach Drives over Wild Moorland and through the finest Coast Scenery in the British Isles.
☞ **The cheapest and most convenient method of seeing the charming West Country.**

WEEK-END TICKETS (all classes)
Are issued every Friday, Saturday, and *Sunday, all the year round to the principal Seaside and Inland Resorts, available for return on the *Sunday, Monday or Tuesday.
* Where train service permits.

EXCURSION TICKETS
Available for from 4 to 18 days, are issued during the Summer, from London (Waterloo) and Provincial towns to nearly all Stations in Devon and North Cornwall.

| CORRIDOR RESTAURANT-CAR EXPRESSES from London (Waterloo) to most places in Devon & N. Cornwall. | THROUGH TICKETS from principal towns in the Midlands and North . . of England . . Ask for tickets "via L. & S.W. Rly." |

For particulars of Train Service, Cheap Tickets, etc., also Illustrated Booklet, " BY THE CORNISH SEA—Holidays in King Arthur's Land," write to Mr. HENRY HOLMES, Supt. of the Line, Waterloo Station, London, S.E.

H. A. WALKER, *General Manager.*

St Ervan, Cornwall

On a bicycle jaunt into the Cornish countryside, John met the rector of St Ervan, who introduced him to Arthur Machen's novel *The Secret Glory*.

> *So, coasting down*
> *In the cool shade of interlacing boughs,*
> *I found St Ervan's partly ruined church,*
> *Its bearded Rector, holding in one hand*
> *A gong-stick, in the other hand a book,*
> *Struck, while he read, a heavy-sounding bell,*
> *Hung from an elm-bough by the churchyard gate.*
> *'Better come in. It's time for Evensong.'*

SUMMONED BY BELLS

'Saint Endellion! Saint Endellion! The name is like a ring of bells.' John was fond of this Cornish church, and one of his granddaughters was christened 'Endellion' there. He especially liked the bell-ringers' rhyme in the tower, painted on a board. 'It shows Georgian ringers in knee breeches and underneath is written a rhyme which ends with these fine four lines:

> *Let's all in love and Friendship hither come*
> *Whilst the shrill treble calls to thundering Tom*
> *And since bells are for modest recreation*
> *Let's rise and ring and fall to admiration.'*

27

St Endellion, Cornwall

Trebetherick was a quiet seaside village. At first the Betjemanns stayed in a rented house; later, Ernest Betjemann built a house there, 'Undertown', designed by the architect Robert Atkinson, who also, surprisingly, designed the showy entrance hall of the *Daily Express* building in Fleet Street.

. . . out of Derry's stable came the brake
To drag us up those long, familiar hills,
Past haunted woods and oil-lit farms and on
To far Trebetherick by the sounding sea.

Summoned by Bells

The first place the Betjemanns stayed in Trebetherick was a boarding-house called The Haven. Another guest there was Joan Larkworthy (later, Mrs Kunzer) whom he later called, in a written book dedication, 'my oldest friend'. She first met John in 1910 when he was four and she was five. 'I can remember to this day the arrival of the Betjemanns. I was frightfully quizzy to know who was coming – peering about. The first one I saw was Bess Betjemann. She always bustled about tremendously: John used to walk exactly like her, rather fast. And then this little thing – I can see him now – coming in in a white suit, little anxious face, big eyes.'

Do you remember, Joan, the awkward time
When we were non-co-operative at sports,
Refusing to be organized in heats?
And when at last we were, and had to race
Out to low-tide line and then back again,
A chocolate biscuit was the only prize?
I laughed. Miss Tunstall sent me home to bed.
You laughed, but not so loudly, and escaped.

Summoned by Bells

John with a favourite aunt, Miss Elsie Avril, and his teddy bear Archibald in Cornwall, about 1913.

Joan Kunzer (*left*) with Mrs Peggy Thomas

Not far down the coast was Polzeath. In the pony-cart is Mr Burden, the local postman.

My father smiled:
'And how's our budding bard? Let what you write
Be funny, John, and be original.'
Secretly proud, I showed off merrily.
But certain as the stars above the twigs
And deeply fearful as the pealing bells
And everlasting as the racing surf
Blown back upon itself in Polzeath Bay,
My urge was to encase in rhythm and rhyme
The things I saw and felt (I could not think).

SUMMONED BY BELLS

POLZEATH BEACH

573 Rock Hotel, from the Beach

WHERE TO STAY AT ROCK.

ROCK HOTEL,

Rock, WADEBRIDGE.

Telegrams : ROCK HOTEL., WADEBRIDGE.

Special Terms for Golfers.   Under
New Management.   Re-decorated
throughout.   Facing Sea.   Close
to Excellent Beaches.   Four minutes'
walk of the famous St. Enodoc Golf
Links.   Fishing and Shooting.
Drawing Room, Coffee, and Smoke
Rooms.

Charges very Moderate.   Bracing Climate

Apply—**MRS. POLLARD, Proprietress,**
Late of Molesworth Hotel, Wadebridge.

PHOTO
CLAUDE HARRIS   MISS VIOLET LORAINE.   252.D.
BEAGLE'S POSTCARDS.

The village of Rock was also near Trebetherick.
Violet Loraine, who made famous the song 'If you
were the only boy in the world and I were the only
girl', had a house there. Ernest Betjemann's friends
John and Eric Asprey, owners of the London store,
used to stay at the Rock Hotel for the golf. After one
of these holidays, Eric Asprey gave John a lift back to
London in his snub-nosed Bentley. He remembers
John, who was still a schoolboy, leaning over the
dashboard and shouting 'Faster! Faster!'

Trebetherick was in the chapelry of St Enodoc (parish of St Minver). For several generations the little church of St Enodoc, with its bent spire like a crooked witch's hat, was almost overwhelmed with sand, and was known locally as 'Sinkininney Church'. But in 1863 the church was dug out and restored. The Revd Sabine Baring-Gould made this digging-out a central episode in his novel *In the Roar of the Sea*, which John enjoyed as a child.

A tablet to the memory of Ernest Betjemann is inside the church; John and his mother are buried in the churchyard.

Come on! come on! This hillock hides the spire,
Now that one and now none. As winds about
The burnished path through lady's finger, thyme
And bright varieties of saxifrage,
So grows the tinny tenor faint or loud
And all things draw towards St Enodoc . . .

SUNDAY AFTERNOON SERVICE IN ST ENODOC
CHURCH, CORNWALL

John took up golf on the St Enodoc links. Irredeemably unsporty, he never became very accomplished, but could occasionally be exhilarated by the game.

How straight it flew, how long it flew,
It clear'd the rutty track
And soaring, disappeared from view
Beyond the bunker's back –
A glorious, sailing, bounding drive
That made me glad I was alive.

SEASIDE GOLF

His poem 'The Hon. Sec.' is a threnody for Ned Burden, secretary of the St Enodoc golf club.

The Harbour, Padstow   Valentine's Series

From the St Enodoc golf links you could see Padstow, reached by rail or ferry. John preferred the ferry: 'We would dip our hands in the water and pretend to feel seasick with each heave of the boat and then the town would spread out before us, its slate roofs climbing up the hillside from the wooden wharves of the harbour until they reached the old church tower . . .' Shopping in Padstow was excitingly different from trailing behind his mother in Kentish Town; and more than once John witnessed the pagan ceremony of the 'obby 'oss, a man in a weird mask and huge hooped tarpaulin skirt, which greets the coming of summer.

Some think of the farthest away places as Spitzbergen or Honolulu. But give me Padstow, though I can reach it any day from Waterloo without crossing the sea. For Padstow is in Cornwall and Cornwall is another country.

FIRST AND LAST LOVES

See once more
The Padstow ferry, worked by oar and sail,
Her outboard engine always going wrong,
Ascend the slippery quay's up-ended slate,
The sea-weed hanging from the harbour wall.
Hot was the pavement under, as I gazed
At lanterns, brass, rope and ships' compasses
In the marine-store window on the quay,
The shoe-shop in the square was cool and dark.
The Misses Quintrell, fancy stationers,
Had most to show me – dialect tales in verse
Published in Truro (Netherton and Worth)
And model lighthouses of serpentine.

SUMMONED BY BELLS

Joan Kunzer (Larkworthy) recalled that John used to force himself to undergo the terrifying ordeal of trespassing in Shilla Woods, which belonged to Captain Rendell. The nearby watermill, Shilla Mill, also had a sinister fascination for John and his friends.

From where the coastguard houses stood
   One used to see, below the hill,
The lichened branches of a wood
   In summer silver-cool and still;
And there the Shade of Evil could
   Stretch out at us from Shilla Mill.

TREBETHERICK

Left to right: Joc Lynam; Vasey, Ralph and Alastair Adams; John Walsham

He fell in love with Biddy, who in this photograph, beside her brother John (a future admiral), has a look of Penelope Chetwode whom John Betjeman married.

His love for Biddy burgeoned at dances in Cornwall when the two were teenagers.

Over the tamarisks the summer night
Heard Melville Gideon on the gramophone.
*   . . . what, by God, was this –*
This tender, humble, unrequited love
For Biddy Walsham? What the worshipping
That put me off my supper, fixed my hair
Thick with Anzora for the dance tonight?

SUMMONED BY BELLS

John's childhood friends in Trebetherick included Joc and Audrey Lynam, children of A.E. ('Hum') Lynam, headmaster of the Dragon School; Biddy and John Walsham, children of Admiral Sir John Walsham in Oxford (they were at the Dragon School with John) and Ralph, Vasey and Alastair Adams. The Walshams and Adamses figure in his poem 'Trebetherick', which appeared in *Old Lights for New Chancels* (1940).

Waves full of treasure then were roaring up the beach,
Ropes round our mackintoshes, waders warm and dry,
We waited for the wreckage to come swirling into reach,
Ralph, Vasey, Alastair, Biddy, John and I.

Marlborough

In September 1920, John became a boarder at
Marlborough College, Wiltshire, founded in 1843 as a
school for the sons of Church of England clergymen.
The original building was an adaptation of the
run-down Castle Inn; but two of the houses and the
school Chapel were designed in the 1840s by Edward
Blore.

Doom! Shivering doom! Clutching a leather grip
Containing things for the first night of term –
House-slippers, sponge-bag, pyjams, Common

Prayer,

My health certificate, photographs of home
(Where were my bike, my playbox and my trunk?) –
I walked with strangers down the hill to school.
The town's first gaslights twinkled in the cold.

SUMMONED BY BELLS

John in the Marlborough Officers' Training Corps

Sir Arthur Elton

E. H. Roberts, Marlborough.

Anthony

Sir Arthur Elton, later a distinguished documentary film-maker and historian of the railways, was in John's year at Marlborough. His ancestral home was Clevedon Court, Somerset, where Tennyson stayed and Arthur Hallam's body was brought in 1833. John visited him there and as a result wrote the essay on Clevedon which was published in *First and Last Loves*.

> Clevedon has the most character, the widest diversity of scenery, the fewest really hideous buildings of all the 'seaside' places I have lately visited. It is quiet, mild, medium-sized. . . . Upon that slender cast-iron pier, built in 1869, strode T.E. Brown, the Clifton schoolmaster and poet. . . . Clevedon Court where the Eltons still live is said to be the oldest inhabited house in England. . . . The earliest development is to be found in simple late Georgian houses of stucco washed cream or white. . . . What a comment on our civilization it is that these modest houses actually *beautify* the hillside . . . .

Other contemporaries at Marlborough included the poets Louis MacNeice (photographed, below, in 1946 when he was a BBC Producer) and Bernard Spencer, and the art historians Anthony Blunt (later Keeper of the Queen's Pictures and unmasked as a spy) and Ellis Waterhouse. Waterhouse parodied the many verses John contributed to the school magazine, *The Marlburian*, in a poem signed with the reversed initials 'B.J.' John retaliated with an acrostic on 'Waterhouse, E.K.'

LINES INSPIRED BY REVERSED INITIALS.

by John Betjeman about Waterhouse. E.K. (acrostic).

Who art thou, second Calverly, who last
　Aspired in nonsense uninspired by skill
To crush extravagance, which once was cast
　E'en from thy mighty pen, no doubt at will,
Revealing youth ? As nonsense was the theme
　Happy you were to write of, for the gaze
Of mocking intellectuals, or the dream,
　Unwittingly Swinburnian faults displays.
Spare me ! thou slaughterer in bombastic verse;
　England hath need of thee for more—why waste
Elaborate genius on a rhymster worse,
　Knowing we both have written in poor taste ?

That most Betjemanian of dwellings, the bungalow, was already appearing in his verse in *The Marlburian*, in a ballad titled 'Revenge' which includes the stanza

Around this house some villas stood,
Small bungalows, all made of wood;
'Twas to the house the figure went,
On some fell purpose strongly bent.

John contributed to *The Marlburian* of 17 November 1921 (when he was fifteen) this poem

ODE TO A CHAR-A-BANC

(With profound apologies to the shade
of P.B. Shelley.)

O 'Charabang' thou breath of Tooting's being,
Thou from whose honking presence, in their tens
Are driven, like tramps from a policeman fleeing,

Women and men and dogs and hectic hens –
All the pedestrian multitude; O thou
Who chariotest through mountains, moors and fens

The tripper crowd, who lie both cold and low
Each like a corpse within his seat, until
The 'Azure Belle' from Hammersmith shall blow

Her Klaxon o'er the dusty road, and fill
(Rousing dull tongues that shouting stir the air)
Thy passengers with joy and merry thrill:
Wild motor which art crashing everywhere,
Killing pedestrian pleasure, hear, O hear! . . .

In March 1924 Louis MacNeice's friend John Hilton wrote in his Marlborough diary: 'There's a new college paper coming out for the first time next Saturday called the "Heretick". It is a very high-brow sort of thing I believe. Blunt's got a lot to do with it. He says it is meant to form a focus for the literary talent in the school.' *The Heretick* was a snook-cocking attack on the athletic faction in the school. Founded by Blunt, John Bowle (who designed the covers) and Philip Harding, it was intended 'to express our disapproval of the Establishment generally, of the more out-of-date and pedantic masters, of all forms of organized sport, of the Officers' Training Corps and of all the other features that we hated in school life, not so much the physical discomforts – they were almost taken for granted – but, as you might say, the intellectual discomforts of the school.' (Anthony Blunt, 'From Bloomsbury to Marxism', *Studio International*, November 1973). Only two issues were produced before it was banned by the Master after parental complaints about an article by Blunt on the Wildean theme that there can be no morality in art. John contributed poetry and prose to both issues.

(The chorus rises higher and higher until it becomes a scream in which the dominant words would appear to be "station port" and "Fifteen." Finally a rout of PRODIGIES *enter. They dance round the Recording Angel singing.)*

PRODIGIES' SONG.

Bright blue skies, and now on the river
   Laziness lies in punt and pillows,
Wandering winds make willow leaves shiver,
   But what care we for the wind in the willows?
What care we for the meadows deep
   And the gentle Kennet's silvery hazes?
Life is only a muddle heap
   Of adjectival phrases.

We must sort it and we must cherish
   Dullest work with our stupid laughter,
And grind and grind till our fancies perish,
   And the heart is lost in a dim hereafter.
A dim hereafter of writing on
  'The Middle Voice' till "over-mellow"
We die, a very pedantic don
   —A crusty college fellow.

(Exit Prodigies.)

J B

THE HERETICK

"UPON PHILISTIA WILL I TRIUMPH"

High Street Marlborough   Christopher Hughes

The art master at Marlborough was Christopher
Hughes, who made an accomplished series of
etchings of Marlborough town. He took the boys on
sketching expeditions into the Wiltshire countryside,
giving them precise and rather old-fashioned
instruction in the art of water-colour. His star pupil
was John's friend John Edward Bowle, who won the
Art Cup in 1924. Bowle took the photograph of John
(next page) on one of these sketching jaunts, lying on
his stomach in the long grass and drawing.

> *I used to sketch*
> *Under the tutelage of Mr. Hughes,*
> *Who taught us art and let us speak our minds –*
> *And now how lovely seemed the light and shade*
> *On cob and thatch of Wiltshire cottages.*
> *When trout waved lazy in the clear chalk streams,*
> *Glory was in me as I tried to paint*
> *The stretch of meadow and the line of downs,*
> *Putting in buttercups in bright gamboge,*
> *Ultramarine and cobalt for the sky,*
> *With blotting-paper, while the page was wet,*
> *For cloud effects.*

SUMMONED BY BELLS

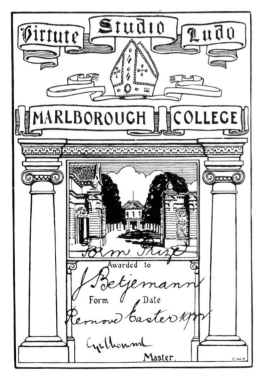

From *The Marlburian*, 12 July 1923

41

John's favourite venue for sketching was Ramsbury Manor, three miles from the school, which had associations with the Meyrick family from which he claimed descent. In the 1970 introduction to the reissue of *Ghastly Good Taste*, he wrote:

> On sketching expeditions I now spurned the old cottages and sought out eighteenth-century buildings. The most beautiful I saw in the neighbourhood was Ramsbury Manor House, a more sophisticated version of Lady Hertford's dwelling at Marlborough. It stood in a landscaped park and could be seen from a bridge across a lake, a gravel drive curling elegantly up to its front door. No words can express my longing to get inside this house, and to see its furniture and library. What the Louvre was to Anthony Blunt and the Parthenon to the boring master who taught us Greek, Ramsbury Manor was to me. I think the mystery of its winding drive gave me a respect for the system of hereditary landowning which I have never shaken off. Christopher Hughes understood this interest in eighteenth-century buildings, and sympathized with my inability to draw Ramsbury and Classical symmetry to my, or his, satisfaction. It also set him and eventually the aesthetes into discussing the merits and demerits of the Victorians.

As at the Dragon School, John excelled in drama at Marlborough. He also won the Furneaux Prize for English Verse, as recorded in *The Marlburian*, 24 July 1925.

SUMMER TERM, 1925.

Carleton Atkinson Spanish Prize—P. A. Mongard.

Curzon Wyllie Memorial Prize—H. C. Hebard.

Drawing Prizes—Lower School, R. P. Kennedy ; extra—A. S. L. Kitching.

English Poetry Prize—T. H. B. Mynors.

Furneaux English Verse Prize—J. Betjemann.

Goodall O.T.C. Prize—N. D. G. Greene.

Kenneth Paul Memorial Gift—C. G. Furnivall.

Masonic Art Cup—C. B. Spencer.

Stephen Reiss Prize—H. J. H. Parker ; commended, T. H. B. Mynors.

Bell Trophy—B1 (Cross Arrows).

At the conclusion of the prize distribution the Musical Society sang four verses of " Carmen Marlburiense."

2103 E   DR. INGRAM
BISHOP OF LONDON.   ROTARY PHOTO. E.C.

Dr Winnington Ingram, the Bishop of London, was an Old Marlburian, and sometimes descended on the school to deliver fulminating sermons in Chapel.

The Old Marlburian bishop thundered on
When all I worshipped were the athletes, ranged
In the pews opposite. 'Be pure,' he cried,
And, for a moment, stilled the sea of coughs.
'Do nothing that would make your mother blush
If she could see you. When the Tempter comes
Spurn him and God will lift you from the mire.'

SUMMONED BY BELLS

On leaving Marlborough in 1925, John and his friends exchanged photographs. Philip Harding was also at Oxford with John and remained a friend until his death in 1972. He lived in Dorset (and is buried there in Shroton churchyard). It was while staying with him one summer holiday that John wrote his poem 'Dorset'. Neville Green was another close friend.

Philip Harding

Neville Green

John's teenage holidays were still spent with his family in Cornwall. Relations were deteriorating with his father, whose arrival in his new Arrol-Johnston car was dreaded.

The Arrol-Johnston spun him down to Slough –
Cornwall the object of the early start
And Newbury a foretaste of the goal,
With Trust House lunch and double Scotch at two . . .

> *Okehampton-wards,*
Through broad red Devon: there's a field of roots,
A covey and an orchard and a farm.
'Its getting late, Bates, switch the headlights on.'
Here, in his deafness and his loneliness,
My father's sad grey eyes in gathering dusk
Saw Roughtor and Brown Willy hide the view
Of that bold coast-line where he was not born . . .

And here was home, and here the gate, and there
The Arrol-Johnston crawling down the lane.
> *And on the morning after burst the storm:*
'How often have I said the bacon's cold?
Confound it, Bess! Confound! When will they learn?'
Bang! Boom! His big fists set the cups a-dance,
The willow-pattern shivered on the shelves . . .

SUMMONED BY BELLS

Oxford

In the autumn of 1925, John became an
undergraduate at Magdalen College, Oxford
(page 65). After the rigours of Marlborough, he
enjoyed his new-found freedom, privacy and luxuries.

Balkan Sobranies in a wooden box,
The college arms upon the lid; Tokay
And sherry in the cupboard; on the shelves
The University Statutes *bound in blue,*
Crome Yellow, Prancing Nigger, *Blunden, Keats.*
My walls were painted Bursar's apple-green;
My wide-sashed windows looked across the grass
To tower and hall and lines of pinnacles.

Summoned by Bells

St Aldate's, Oxford (left) leads down to Tom Tower, Christ Church

While peer and peasant tread the sculptured stair
  The festal light to share
  Of Christ Church hall.
Let the obscure cathedral's organ note
Out, out into the starry darkness float
O'er my friend Auden and the clever men,
Running like mad to miss the upper ten
Who burst from 'Peck' in Bullingdonian brawl,
  Jostling some pale-faced victim, you or me.

SUMMONED BY BELLS

John was an intimate friend of W.H. Auden's at Oxford. Through him he met Christopher Isherwood, the novelist.

W.H. Auden aged 22, by Cecil Beaton

It was the Oxford of plus fours, verandah suits, violet hair cream, Charvet silk ties and open sports cars; shingled hair and slave bangles for the rare fashionable undergraduettes. Bryan Guinness (now Lord Moyne) who preceded John as editor of the *Cherwell*, wrote of 'the gramophonic, cinematographic life of the Oxford set'. On their gramophones the undergraduates played the Black Bottom, 'Chili Bom Bom', 'Oh, Those Naughty Eyes', 'Yes Sir, That's My Baby' and 'Happy Days Are Here Again'. But the fashion for voluminous 'Oxford bags' was passing.

> I came up to the University just as the 'Oxford Bags' were going out. I doubt if they had ever come in with the grand sets in which I aspired to move. The year must have been 1925 when still the tales of Harold Acton, Brian Howard and Cyril Connolly lingered and the few aesthetes of that generation who had not been sent down, were staying on for a final year.
>
> John Betjeman, 'The Silver Age of Aesthetes'
> PARSON'S PLEASURE, 15 October 1958.

'A PAIR OF PANTY LOONS.'

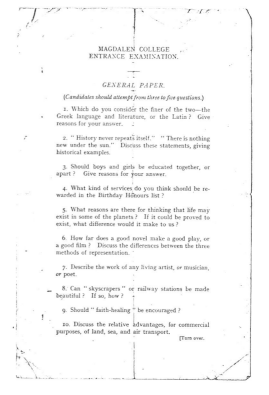

The President of Magdalen was the venerable Sir Herbert Warren (photographed here with Lady Warren in 1926), who had been a Fellow of the college since 1875, President since 1885. A minor poet himself, he had known John's idol, Tennyson. Warren was a celebrated snob. An Indian prince who became an undergraduate at the college said that he was styled 'the son of God' in his country. Warren coughed and said: 'You will find, Your Highness, that we have the sons of many famous fathers here.'

John put a mark against (and presumably answered) question 8 in the general paper of the Magdalen College entrance examination. It was a perfect question for somebody of his architectural interests. All the same, he did not do well in the examination; but Warren exercised his right, as President, to admit him regardless of the examination results – possibly because he liked the poem with which John had won a prize at Marlborough.

John's favourite tutor at Magdalen was the Revd J.M. Thompson, historian of the French Revolution. The Bishop of Winchester had deprived him of his post of Dean of Divinity at the college in 1911, when Thompson had denied the existence of miracles in his book *Miracles in the New Testament*. From the start, John liked and respected this 'shy, kind, amusing man' – 'Thompie', as he called him. Most Sundays, he visited Thompson and his wife Mari Meredyth at their home in Chadlington Road, North Oxford, for tea and talk. John would leave when summoned by the bells of St Barnabas, Oxford:

How long was the peril, how breathless the day,
In topaz and beryl, the sun dies away,
His rays lying static at quarter to six
In polychromatical lacing of bricks.
Good Lord, as the angelus floats down the road,
Byzantine St Barnabas, be Thine abode.

Sᴛ Bᴀʀɴᴀʙᴀs, Oxꜰᴏʀᴅ

Maurice Bowra with Elizabeth and Kitty Harman

John's other great friend among the dons was Maurice Bowra, Dean of Wadham, who was host to a brilliant coterie of undergraduates, including John, Kenneth Clark, Elizabeth Harman (now Lady Longford), Osbert Lancaster, Anthony Powell, John Sparrow and Henry Yorke ('Henry Green').

Dinner with Maurice Bowra sharp at eight –
High up in Wadham's hospitable quad:
The Gilbert Spencers and the Campbell Gray
Bright in the inner room; the brown and green
Of rows and rows of Greek and Latin texts;
The learning lightly worn; the grand contempt
For pedants, traitors and pretentiousness.
A dozen oysters and a dryish hock;
Claret and tournedos; a bombe surprise . . .
The fusillade of phrases ('I'm a man
More dined against than dining') rattled out
In that incisive voice and chucked away
To be re-used in envious common-rooms
By imitation Maurices. I learned,
If learn I could, how not to be a bore,
And merciless was his remark that touched
The tender spot if one were showing off.
Within those rooms I met my friends for life . . .

King of a kingdom underneath the stars,
I wandered back to Magdalen, certain then,
As now, that Maurice Bowra's company
Taught me far more than all my tutors did.

Summoned by Bells

By contrast, John detested – then and for ever – C.S. Lewis (right), his tutor in English Literature. One might have expected these two famous apologists for Church of England Christianity to be natural allies; but while John had already been Summoned by Bells, Lewis had not yet been Surprised by Joy. John hated his sarcasm and his booming voice. To Lewis, John was a frivolous playboy, who came to some tutorials in carpet slippers and cut others with unconvincing excuses. When John was about to leave Oxford after failing in Divinity, 'I sought my tutor in his arid room, Who told me, "You'd have only got a Third".' John took revenge on Lewis in his poems and other writings.

Oh! well-bound Wells and Bridges! Oh! earnest
ethical search
For the wide high-table λογος of St. C.S. Lewis's
Church.

May-Day Song for North Oxford

Maurice Bowra: a pencil portrait by Henry Lamb, 1931

Bowra's main rival as an Oxford host was 'Colonel' George Kolkhorst, a lecturer in Spanish – he was invested with a mythical colonelcy in the Portuguese Medical Corps because he looked so unlike a colonel. His undergraduate friends, including John, came to his rooms in Beaumont Street at about 12.30 on Sundays. The rooms contained Victoriana under glass domes, Japanese prints, a photograph of Walter Pater, and suits of Japanese armour in which, according to Osbert Lancaster, families of mice had made their homes. Those who were in the colonel's good books were given sherry, those who had in some way offended him, marsala. After a few glasses, singing, chanting and other entertainment began.

We bought the Sunday newspapers and rush'd
Down Beaumont Street to Number 38
And Colonel Kolkhorst's Sunday-morning rout,

> *D'ye ken Kolkhorst in his artful parlour,*
> *Handing out the drink at his Sunday morning gala?*
> *Some get sherry and some get Marsala –*
> *With his arts and his crafts in the morning!*

Summoned by Bells

Kolkhorst is in the centre of the top right-hand window in Osbert Lancaster's cartoon, John second from the left in the adjoining window.

One of the first people John met at Magdalen was Martyn Skinner, who arrived as a freshman on the same day. Skinner recalls: 'Some of us were waiting in the Magdalen cloisters to go into Hall to dinner, when he came along cloisters shouting these lines from Jean Ingelow's "The High Tide on the Coast of Lincolnshire":

"Cusha! Cusha! Cusha!" calling,
Ere the early dews were falling,
Farre away I heard her song,
"Cusha! Cusha!" all along.

I can still hear him shouting it.' In 1941 John reviewed in the *Oxford Magazine* Skinner's long poem *Letters to Malaya*, which won the Hawthornden Prize; and in 1966 he found a publisher for his epic poem *The Return of Arthur*, in which John is mentioned. In 1961 John addressed a poem to Skinner, later published in *High and Low* (1966).

Martyn Skinner: portrait by Eric Kennington RA

Eric Walter White (later a world authority on Stravinsky and a senior official of the Arts Council of Great Britain) was at Balliol. When John was editor of *Cherwell*, the university magazine, he published several of White's poems. The two had something else in common: both spent their holidays in Cornwall. John was fascinated by White's triple name. To the same issue of *Cherwell* in which he published White's poem 'Min' in 1927, John contributed this verse:

CHELTENHAM

Eric Walter White
Walter Thursby Pelham
The Montpelier Rotunda
received them under
its Tuscan Order
White and Waite wait
for Walter Thursby Pelham
in Montpelier Rotunda.

White did not realize John was the author. But almost twenty years later, when they met at a Hampstead party, John recited the whole poem at him.

John's best friend at Magdalen was Lionel Perry (above right), who had come up to Oxford the year before him. He was rich, handsome and witty. From his blond hair and unfading suntan, he was known as 'the golden boy'. His father was Fred ('Peter') Perry, a Fellow of All Souls who had been a member of Lord Milner's 'Kindergarten'.

Michael Dugdale (below), at Balliol, was another prominent aesthete. His mother, Blanche ('Baffie') Dugdale, was the niece and biographer of Balfour, the Prime Minister. He became an architect and in the 1930s was a member of the avant-garde architectural group Tecton, which designed the Highpoint I flats in Highgate and the penguin pool and the gorilla house at London Zoo.

Come, Michael Arthur Stratford Dugdale, rise
*   And Lionel Geoffrey Perry. It is ten.*
Binsey to Cowley, Oxford open lies.
*   They breakfasted at eight, the college men*
Who will be pouring out of lectures when
*   Eleven strikes . . .*
*   Rise! we ourselves are pledged to drink with Ben.*

S<small>UMMONED BY</small> B<small>ELLS</small>

Lionel Perry had known John Dugdale (no relation of Michael) since the age of thirteen: they had been at school together. It was through John's introduction to Dugdale by Perry that he came to stay in his first great English house, for Dugdale lived at Sezincote, Gloucestershire, a palace in Indian style designed for Sir Charles Cockerell about 1805 by his brother, the architect Samuel Pepys Cockerell. Sezincote became John's second home: in the dedication of his first book, *Mount Zion* (1931), to John Dugdale's mother Ethel, he wrote: 'Constantly under these minarets I have been raised from the deepest depression and spent the happiest days of my life'.

Oxford May mornings! When the prunus bloomed
We'd drive to Sunday lunch at Sezincote:
First steps in learning how to be a guest,
First wood-smoke-scented luxury of life
In the large ambience of a country house. . . .

SUMMONED BY BELLS

Colonel Dugdale with his war veteran mare at Sezincote.

The love between those seeming opposites,
Colonel and Mrs Dugdale, warmed their guests.
The paddock where the Colonel's favourite mare,
His tried companion of the '14 war,
Grazed in retirement – what is in it now?

SUMMONED BY BELLS

John at Sezincote with Colin Gill, later Rector of St Magnus-the-Martyr, City of London

SHELTON ABBEY, ARKLOW

Lionel Perry also introduced John to Lord Clonmore, son of the seventh Earl of Wicklow. 'Billy' Clonmore was an ordinand at St Stephen's House in Norham Road, North Oxford. John's Marlborough/Balliol friend John Bowle said Clonmore 'looked exactly like the Mad Hatter: he *was* the Mad Hatter.' Evelyn Waugh wrote of him that his 'extravagances were refined by a slightly antiquated habit of speech and infused with a Christian piety that was unique among us and lay hidden behind his stylish eccentricities.' John stayed with Clonmore at the Wicklows' home, Shelton Abbey, a Gothick mansion near Arklow, Ireland. When Clonmore (by now Earl of Wicklow) died in 1978, John wrote to Lionel Perry: 'You must have been through agony as Crax [pet name for Wicklow] was a saint, the only *certain* one I knew.'

Robert Byron was a friend of Clonmore's: they had been in the same house at Eton, with Oliver Messel. John's and Byron's undergraduate days only overlapped for one term, but Byron was one of the most frequent revenants to Oxford, making appearances at Bowra's and Kolkhorst's salons. Byron influenced John's taste and prose style profoundly (he was an early enthusiast for Victoriana); and it was through him, too, that John met his future wife Penelope Chetwode.

R. Byron.

Harold Acton, who also belonged to the slightly earlier Oxford of Evelyn Waugh, had grown up in a baroque Florentine palazzo. He knew Max Beerbohm, D.H. Lawrence, Ronald Firbank and Aldous Huxley. His first book of poems, *Aquarium*, was published during his second term in 1923. John recalled that Acton 'was never seen inside the college [Christ Church] in my day. He was a frequenter of restaurants, and his own lodgings were somewhere in the High.' Acton remembers: 'We became friends at first sight. John looked as if he had tumbled out of bed and dressed in a hurry, necktie askew and shoe-laces undone, while a school bell seemed to be tinkling in the distance. A boy scout out of uniform, with Ruskin as his Baden-Powell.'

John Sutro was another survivor of the Waugh years who became a friend of John's. Waugh wrote of him in *A Little Learning*:

> . . . He has with age changed little in appearance, which was always singular and endearing, like a creation of Waterton's; as though a whimsical taxidermist had secured some transitional anthropoid specimen, stripped it of its outer hide and replaced it with the skin of a rosy and robust baby, crowned the head with a soft brown wig and set it with large, innocent blue eyes, taken, one might think, from one of the Mitford sisters.

In the mid 1930s John Betjeman and John Sutro starred in a film together (see page 108).

'To-morrow to fresh woods and pastures new.'—H.A. and P.J.M. prepare to depart from Oxford.

Tom Driberg, who had been at Lancing with Evelyn Waugh, had many poems published in the *Cherwell*, and took over from Harold Acton and Brian Howard the role of poetical and surrealist impresario of Oxford. He brought Edith Sitwell and the French surrealist poet René Crevel to the city. Later, as the first 'William Hickey' of the *Daily Express*, he gave publicity to the young Betjeman. With John Sparrow he remained one of the two friends whose advice on his poetry (including extensive suggestions for changes in words and lines) John most welcomed.

I should think that giggling and irresponsible period, before the slump and the serious 'thirties, is typified by a performance in the Music Rooms in Holywell. It was called 'Homage to Beethoven' and so a nice collection of old ladies from North Oxford in silk shawls was present. The music, which had typewriters in it, was by Archie Gwynne Brown. The words were by Tom Driberg.

If I forget thee, Sion, Sion,
May all my members lose their skill,

one section began, ending with lines something like these:–

. . . a naked phallus beckons,
In blushing starkness from the hill

and so on until the climax which was the flushing of a lavatory situated just behind the stage.

John Betjeman, 'The Silver Age of Aesthetes', Parson's Pleasure, 15 October 1958

Alan Pryce-Jones (photographed, above, in 1933 with Joan Eyres Monsell), the future editor of *The Times Literary Supplement*, arrived at Magdalen in 1927, the beginning of John's third year there. He recalls their first meeting: 'I was wearing a dressing-gown on my way to the very remote bathroom which one had in those days, about half a mile from one's rooms in college; and John thought it such a curious dressing-gown – it was kind of cape-shaped – that he suddenly said "What are you doing wearing that extraordinary garment?" and we made friends from that point.' Pryce-Jones lived in Chelsea – not far from John in Old Church Street. The two often met in the vacations and got to know each other's families. Immediately after Oxford, Pryce-Jones joined the staff of the *London Mercury* under (Sir) John Squire, who published John's short story 'Lord Mount Prospect' and some of his poems.

Alan Pryce-Jones came in a bathing-dress
And, seated at your low harmonium,
Struck up the Kolkhorst Sunday-morning hymn:
'There's a home for Colonel Kolkhorst' – final verse
ff with all the stops out. . . .

Summoned by Bells

Another regular at Beaumont Street and friend of Lionel Perry was Graham Eyres Monsell. He was a member of the 'Georgeoisie' – those who habitually dined at the St George Restaurant on the Cornmarket and George Street, 'where punkahs, suspended from the ceiling, swayed to and fro, dispelling the smoke of Egyptian and Balkan cigarettes'. He and his beautiful sister Joan (now Mrs Patrick Leigh Fermor) were children of the First Lord of the Admiralty, 'Bobby' (Sir Bolton, later Lord, Monsell). John visited the Eyres Monsells at their family home, Dumbleton House, Evesham, and wrote three poems about it, two in Longfellow style, the third a nonsense-poem in which Alan Pryce-Jones (known as 'Boggins') and Sir Bolton Eyres Monsell both figure:

John at Dumbleton, 1933: 'the author – an example of good taste, if ever there was one' (his own words)

Dumbleton, Dumbleton, the ruin by the lake,
*   Where Boggins and Sir Bolton fought a duel*
*   for thy sake;*
Dumbleton, Dumbleton, the Gothic arch that leads
*   Thro' the silver vestibule to where*
*   Sir Bolton feeds.*
*   The groaning of the golden plate,*
*   The sickly social shame;*
*   Oh heirs of Dumbleton! The Monsell in thy name!*

SEEN IN THE GEORGE. Nos. 5 and 6.

Caricature of Robin Morrison and Graham Eyres Monsell by Osbert Lancaster, *Isis*, 6 June 1928

Messrs. R-b-n M-rr-s-n and Gr-h-m E-r-s-Mo-ns-ll.

John Edward Bowle, John's Marlborough contemporary, had won a Brackenbury scholarship at Balliol. He disappointed his tutors by obtaining only a Third in the History schools; though in later life he became a well-known historian. He shared London lodgings with John in the early 1930s, when a young master at Westminster School. The novelist Angus Wilson, who was one of his pupils there, remembers that when Bowle got slightly tipsy one evening, John Betjeman, who was present, stood on a table and addressed the boys, in the language of a public-school novel: 'Now you fellows won't peach on John Edward, will you?'

John Edward Bowle
Will bring his soul.

SUMMONED BY BELLS

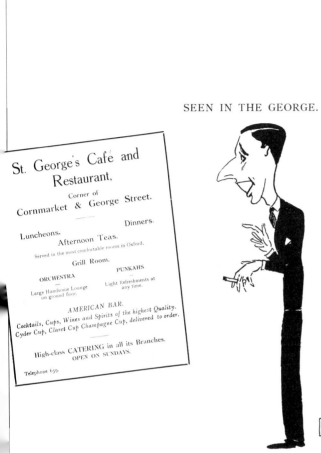

SEEN IN THE GEORGE.

St. George's Café and Restaurant,
Corner of
Cornmarket & George Street.

Luncheons.   Dinners.
        Afternoon Teas.
    Served in the most comfortable rooms in Oxford.

        Grill Room.

ORCHESTRA   PUNKAHS

Large Handsome Lounge   Light Refreshments at
   on ground floor.   any time.

        AMERICAN BAR.
Cocktails, Cups, Wines and Spirits of the highest Quality.
Cyder Cup, Claret Cup Champagne Cup, delivered to order.

High-class CATERING in all its Branches.
        OPEN ON SUNDAYS.

Telephone 659.

MR. TH--D-R- Y-T-S.

Caricature by Osbert Lancaster, *Isis*, 24 May 1928

Theodore Yates (he had dropped his original name, Jack) was another member of the Georgeoisie. John was to become a close friend of his when they worked together for the British Council at Blenheim Palace in 1946; later, when Yates had set up an antiquarian bookshop in his home town of Louth, Lincolnshire, he introduced John to the church described in John's poem 'A Lincolnshire Church'. At Oxford Yates was also a friend of the historian A.J.P. Taylor, though Taylor says in his autobiography that they had 'nothing in common except a liking for each other's company'.

SEEN IN THE GEORGE. No. VII.

J-HN -DW-RD B-WL-

Caricature by Osbert Lancaster, *Isis*, 21 June 1928

THE 'JELLYFISH' AT WORK.

Caricature, *Isis*, 16 February 1928

Oxford was divided into Aesthetes and Hearties. The aesthetes were languid, elegantly or bizarrely dressed and predominantly homosexual. The athletes perpetuated the sportiness of their public schools and enjoyed rough horseplay such as breaking up aesthetes' rooms or smashing windows. Some of them liked girls, too: and there were protests in the *Isis* about 'the Jellyfish' who would sit, uninvited, next to girls in the Super Cinema and press their attentions on them. John regarded himself as an aesthete, and on one occasion his Magdalen rooms were wrecked by hearties.

There was one college, Brasenose, which was entirely hearty and dangerous for any aesthete to enter wearing the usual badges of his party – a shantung silk tie, lavender trousers, orange, red or saxe blue shirt. A friend of mine, Michael Dugdale, always entered it limping as he thought the hearties would be too sporting to attack a fellow athlete.

John Betjeman, 'The Silver Age of Aesthetes', PARSON'S PLEASURE, 15 October 1958

THIS WEEK IN THE GARDEN.

LILIES.
They toil not, neither do they spin ;
They're pure without—but not within.

Caricature by Osbert Lancaster, *Isis*, 8 June 1927

One of the most extreme aesthetes of the 1920s was Edouard Roditi of Balliol, who overlapped with John by only one term in 1928 but knew him as a revenant, as John had known Harold Acton and Evelyn Waugh. The Master of Balliol (the Socialist Alexander Lindsay) was quoted in *Cherwell* of 1 December 1928 as declaring: 'Mr Roditi, you are the second Harold Acton and the third Oscar Wilde.' Through his father, who ran a big export business, Roditi knew John's father Ernest. He was at Charterhouse with Osbert Lancaster, who called him 'an infant Dadaist' in his memoirs. Roditi later wrote a biography of Magellan; edited the Penguin anthology of surrealism; and became a distinguished translator.

Lennox Berkeley, the composer, also affected the aesthete's uniform at this date. He was to be a friend of John's later years, too, as a member of what John called 'the Paddington Set', with Patrick Kinross and Lady Diana Cooper.

Edouard Roditi

Edward James, who was to be the private publisher, in 1931, of John's first book of poetry, *Mount Zion*, was one of the wealthiest men in Oxford in John's time. King Edward VII was his godfather, and just possibly his father. His rooms in Christ Church were celebrated for their luxurious and avant-garde decor. John persuaded him to put money into the ailing *Cherwell*. Later James became a patron and collector of the surrealists. By the time *Summoned by Bells* was published in 1960, he was living in Mexico, where he had designed some extraordinary buildings in the jungle.

On tapestries from Brussels looms
  The low late-'20s sunlight falls
In those black-ceilinged Oxford rooms
  And on their silver-panelled walls;
ARS LONGA VITA BREVIS EST
Was painted on them – not in jest. . . .

They tell me he's in Mexico,
  They will not give me his address;
But if he sees this book he'll know
  I do not value him the less.
For Art is long and Life must end,
My earlier publisher and friend.

SUMMONED BY BELLS

Lennox Berkeley

Christopher Sykes, later to be Evelyn Waugh's biographer, helped John to run the *Cherwell*. He was to marry Camilla Russell (who had formerly been engaged, briefly, to John). Sykes respected John, though he viewed him as an eccentric. 'I remember one thing that was odd about him,' he recalled. 'When he passed a building he admired, he used to clap.' Sykes was involved with John in one of John's earliest preservation campaigns: the attempt to save from destruction the Radcliffe Observatory, Oxford, designed by Wyatt. It had outlived its usefulness as an observatory. John's characteristic tone of scathing irony is heard in his caption to a picture of the Observatory (after a painting by J. Dixon, 1791) which appeared in the supplement to the *Cherwell* on 25 June 1927:

> The Radcliffe Observatory. How right that Oxford's loveliest building is closed to the public. With acknowledgements to the Visitors of the Ashmolean Museum.

The Observatory was saved. The illustration here is by Thomas Rowlandson, *c.* 1810.

RANDOLPH HOTEL

IN THE CENTRE OF THE CITY.

THE MODERN HOTEL OF OXFORD. Near Colleges, Public Buildings, and opposite the Martyrs' Memorial. Every comfort and convenience. Handsome Suites of Rooms. Drawing Rooms. New Lounges. Smoking and Billiard Rooms. Garage adjoining. Night Porter in attendance.

UP-TO-DATE CENTRAL HEATING.

Electric Elevator.   Moderate Charges.   R.A C., and A.A.
Telephone No. 290 Oxford   Address : THE MANAGERESS.

Osbert Lancaster came up to Lincoln College in October 1926 and quickly became a friend of John's, possibly through Graham Shepard, also of Lincoln, who had been at Marlborough with John. (The son of E.H. Shepard, illustrator of A.A. Milne's 'Pooh' books, Graham Shepard, like John, owned a teddy-bear destined to immortality: his was the model for the 'Pooh' drawings.) John and Osbert Lancaster already shared an interest in the Victorians: in 1927 Lancaster contributed a series to the *Cherwell* – 'Little Known Gems of Victorian Art', and the two men remained lifelong friends. Lancaster drew the 'pocket cartoon' in the *Daily Express* for over forty years. In the Randolph Hotel, Oxford, he executed a series of murals illustrating Max Beerbohm's Oxford novel *Zuleika Dobson*.

John's poem 'The Church's Restoration' first appeared in the *Isis* of 24 October 1928, under another title. Mowbray's, the church furnishing firm, complained about the reference to them in stanza five: in modern editions, the line has been changed to 'Sing art and crafty praise'.

Mr. OSBERT LANCASTER.

To the Blessed St. Aubin

*(To be sung, as reverently as possible, to the tune of
' The Church's One Foundation.')*

The church's restoration
  In eighteen-eighty-three
Has left for contemplation
  Not what there used to be.

How well the ancient woodwork
  Looks round the rectory hall,
Memorial of the good work
  Of him who planned it all.

He who took down the pew-ends,
  And sold them anywhere,
And kindly spared a few ends
  Worked up into a chair.

A worthy persecution
  Of dust ! Oh hue divine,
Oh cheerful substitution,
  Thou varnishèd pitch-pine.

Church furnishing ! Church furnishing !
  Come, Mowbray, swell the praise !
He gave the brass for burnishing,
  He gave the thick red baize.

He gave the new addition,
  Pulled down the dull old aisle ;
To pave the Sweet Transition
  He gave th' encaustic tile.

Of marble brown and veinèd
  He did the pulpit make,
He ordered windows stainèd,
  Light red and crimson lake.

Sing on with hymns uproarious,
  Ye humble and aloof ;
Look up, and oh, how glorious !
  He has renewed the roof.   J.B.

The Sitwells and T.S. Eliot were the poets most admired by the avant-garde Oxford undergraduate writers; but Kipling, Chesterton and Belloc, and John Masefield were pillars of the more orthodox literary establishment, and had more influence on John's poetry. Betjeman introduced a selection of Masefield's poems in 1978.

The caricatures below are by Bert Thomas from *Meet These People* by Reginald Arkell (Herbert Jenkins, 1928).

Mr. PETER FLEMING, the Editor.
'Pithecanthropus' to his friends.

J. FERNALD

GRISEWOOD

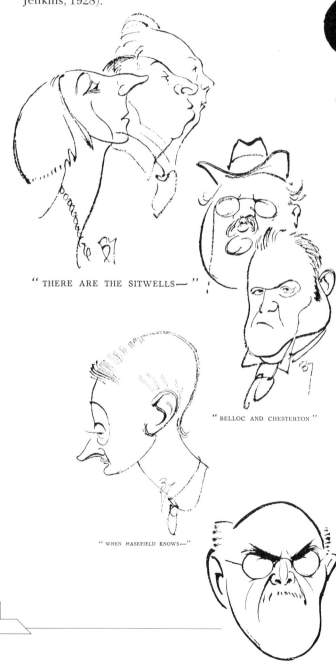

" THERE ARE THE SITWELLS— "

" BELLOC AND CHESTERTON "

" WHEN MASEFIELD KNOWS— "

" KIPLING'S TALES ARE STILL THE BEST "

John took part in Magdalen College drama productions and was a peripheral figure in the Oxford University Dramatic Society, where his Wart and porter in *Henry IV Part II* won praise in 1926. J.B. Fagan cast him as Starveling in his production of *A Midsummer Night's Dream* in the same year. Among his OUDS friends were the god-like Gyles Isham of Magdalen, John Fernald, who had been at Marlborough with him, Emlyn Williams and (later) Ian Fleming's brother Peter; though Harman Grisewood was one of those who insisted on John's expulsion from the OUDS after John, as editor of the *Cherwell*, had published a spoof photograph of the OUDS rehearsing, with ribald caption.

Suddenly, this year, the club [OUDS] seemed less inhibited, more whimsical, and hadn't people got less tall, more my size? I scanned them. They all looked more like promoted school-fellows than Ouds members: a bouncing fresh-faced head boy biting a pipe named J.B. Fernald, a gentle fag of a Pat Moynihan, a languid cherub in plus-fours (Martin Rellander), a fair quiet school captain with a diffident repose (Charles Garvenal), a hesitant moon-calf (Douglas Cleverdon), and a zany wiseacre with a protruding tooth: a fourth-former by the difficult name of Betjeman.

Emlyn Williams, GEORGE, 1961

Magdalen tower from the water-meadows

New Buildings, Magdalen College, Oxford, John's first home in the University

Furness, Naas.

In the vacations, John stayed with Pierce Synnott (left) in his mansion Furness at Naas, Co. Kildare, Ireland. Synnott was regarded as 'a gilded popinjay' by the Master of his College, Balliol, but confounded him by taking a First. John also enjoyed staying with Patrick Balfour (far right, later Lord Kinross) at Traigh Mhór, the Kinrosses' holiday cottage on the island of Iona. Balfour's mother, Lady Kinross (right), became a close friend and *confidante*.

Traigh Mhór.

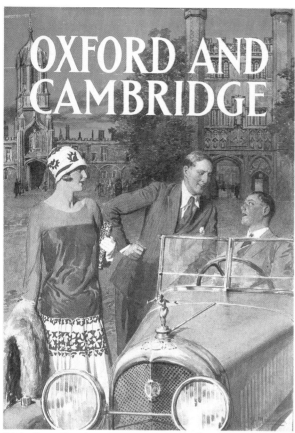

OXFORD AND CAMBRIDGE

Bright Young People in 1927. Most undergraduates in John's time were fee-paying, not on scholarships, and many could afford smart sports cars

Illustration by R.S. Sherriffs of 'The Arrest of Oscar Wilde at the Cadogan Hotel' in *Oxford and Cambridge* magazine, 1933

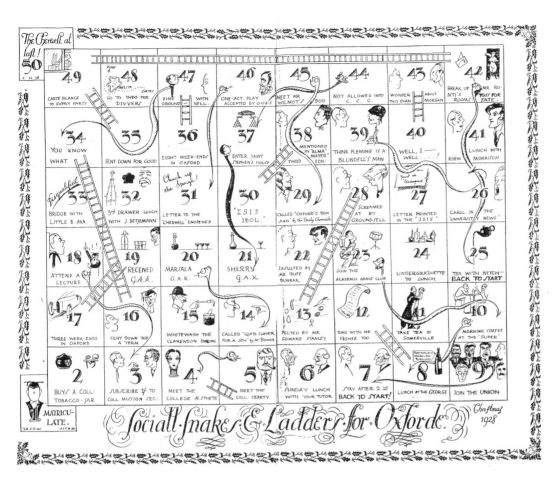

The Cherwell at last! 50

'Sociall Snakes & Ladders for Oxford'. Christmas 1928

'Sociall Snakes & Ladders for Oxford', a spoof board game which appeared in the *Cherwell* of 8 December 1928, offered a '3rd drawer lunch with J. Betjemann' at square 32. Squares 20 and 21 offer marsala and sherry respectively with Colonel G.A. Kolkhorst.

At Oxford, John was an Anglo-Catholic, attending Mass at Pusey House. His religiosity was well-known and inspired this caricature by the young Osbert Lancaster in the *Cherwell*.

Prep School Master

John was rusticated in the summer term of 1928 after failing in the Divinity examination ('Divvers'). Like other Oxford failures before him, he went to Gabbitas-Thring's scholastic agency in quest of a prep school job. (Evelyn Waugh describes the same experience in *Decline and Fall*.) The first job he obtained through them was at Thorpe House School, Gerrard's Cross, run by Mr Noble.

Ah, welcome door, Gabbitas Thring & Co.'s
Scholastic agency in Sackville Street!
'The Principal will see you.' 'No degree?
There is, perhaps, a temporary post
As cricket master for the coming term
At Gerrard's Cross. Fill in this form and give
Qualifications – testimonials
Will help – and if you are accepted, please
Pay our commission promptly. Well, good day!'

SUMMONED BY BELLS

Heddon Court

John, in a Magdalen College blazer,
as an assistant master at Thorpe House School

Among his pupils were the future Sir Jasper Hollom,
Chief Cashier of the Bank of England, the future
Sir John Addis, British Ambassador to China, and
(shown here, left to right), James Orr, who became
private secretary to Prince Philip, Duke of Edinburgh;
Kenric Rice, a director of the Hong Kong and
Shanghai Bank; and Paul Miller, a Canon of Derby
Cathedral.

> *Matron made*
> *A final survey of the boys' best clothes. –*
> *Clean shirts. Clean collars. 'Rice, your jacket's torn.*
> *Bring it to me this instant.'*
>
> CRICKET MASTER

In 1929 John became private secretary to Sir Horace
Plunkett (right), a 75-year-old Irishman whose main
interest was the Irish dairy trade. The appointment
was not a great success, and after a few months John
was replaced as secretary by John Bowle.

> Working in JB is the thing that matters most. The whole
> trouble is that he cannot concentrate on anything.
> He reads a bit of agricultural cooperation stuff and then
> writes a poem or a story which comes much easier than
> my dull drab toil.
>
> *Diary of Sir Horace Plunkett*, 18 February 1929

John's next job, which lasted a little longer, was as a
prep-school master at Heddon Court, Cockfosters,
Hertfordshire.

Most of the Heddon Court boys came from rich families. This is the Renault of Alan Nightingale's family. The masters had less grand cars. One owned a Hupmobile, a car which figures in John's later poem, 'Indoor Games near Newbury' –

Rich the makes of motor whirring,
Past the pine-plantation purring
  Come up, Hupmobile, Delage!
Short the way your chauffeurs travel,
Crunching over private gravel
  Each from out his warm garáge.

John had obtained the job by pretending he was good at cricket. In fact he had to mug up the places on the field from a *Letts Schoolboys' Diary*, and was soon shown up as a hopeless duffer on the field.

Vainly I tried to fend the hail of balls
Hurled at my head by brutal Barnstaple
And at my shins by Winters. Nasty quiet
Followed my performance. When the sun
Had sunk behind the fringe of Hadley Wood
And Barnstaple and I were left alone
Among the ash-trays of the common-room,
He murmured in his soft West-country tones:
'D'you know what Winters told me, Betjeman?
He didn't think you'd ever held a bat.'

CRICKET MASTER

Alan Nightingale and his father at Heddon Court

John and friend at Heddon Court, *c.* 1930

John made friends with the gym mistress, Vera Spencer-Clarke. He wrote love poems to her, which neither took too seriously, as she was engaged to another master, Walter Moule, who was away in Africa. John attended her wedding (the photograph also shows the school's headmaster, John Humphrey Hope, who was a communist and used to make soap-box speeches in Hyde Park. Under his influence, John temporarily became a 'parlour pink'.) Years later, Vera Moule made a bronze bust of John.

Vera Spencer-Clarke is married
And the rest are dead and buried;
I am thirty summers older,
Richer, wickeder and colder,
Fuller too of care . . .

CRICKET MASTER

One evening John, Vera and another master called Huxtable ('Barnstaple' in John's poem) drove to a pub for a drink. On the way back, Huxtable drove over the school's holy-of-holies, the cricket pitch, and he was sacked. John stayed for a few more terms.

The more we sang, the faster Barnstaple
Drove his old Morris, swerving down the drive
And in and out of rhododendron clumps,
Over the very playing-field itself,
And then – oh horror! – right across the pitch
Not once, but twice or thrice. The mark of tyres
Next day was noticed at the Parents' Match.

CRICKET MASTER

With The Bright Young People

One of John's pupils, Dick Addis (brother of John) invited him to Scotland for the holidays, to Hartrigge, near Jedburgh. They swam in the River Jed and John told ghost stories in the great hall. There John met the Addises' sister Margie (seen here in Court presentation dress in 1929), who was to be a lifelong friend. John's hair was considered very long. Before they visited some rather grand neighbours, she offered to cut it with a pair of nail scissors. John agreed. When they arrived at the grand house, Margie Addis was taken aside and asked: 'What is wrong with your friend Mr Betjeman? Has he got the *mange*?'

Camilla Russell by Devas

During the holidays and at some weekends, John managed to sustain his high-flying social life. At Sezincote he met the beautiful Camilla Russell, who lived nearby at Little Compton. At one time he became engaged to her, but Camilla's father, Russell Pasha, who had been head of the police in Cairo, insisted the engagement be broken off after he discovered a copy of James Hanley's novel *Boy* which John had sent her.

Osbert Lancaster, Camilla Russell, and Guy Powell

'Betjeman returns to London'

John at Little Compton

Russell Pasha in playful pose

Sir Henry d'Avigdor-Goldsmid was one of the richest men at Oxford in John's time. He held lavish parties on his steam yacht. After Oxford, friends such as John were often invited for the weekend to his home, Somerhill, Kent. In later years, John was fond of quoting one of d'Avigdor-Goldsmid's maxims: 'Good news seldom arrives in a buff envelope.'

This Somerhill house-party of 1930 includes several of John's friends: *back row, left to right*: Basil Burton, Randolph Churchill, Mrs d'Avigdor Goldsmid, Nancy Goldsmid, Julian Goldsmid, Osmond D'A. Goldsmid; *middle row, left to right*: Christopher Hobhouse, Pamela Nathan, Clarissa Goldsmid, Elizabeth Harman (now Lady Longford), J. d'A. Goldsmid; *front row, left to right*: Rosamund Fisher, Patrick Balfour (later Lord Kinross), Diana Churchill, Johnnie Churchill, Henry d'A. Goldsmid, Tony Goldsmid.

Frank and Elizabeth Pakenham (now the Earl and Countess of Longford) married at St Margaret's Westminster in 1931. John stayed with them several times at their first home, Stairways, at Stone, near Aylesbury. An open-air performance of hymns was staged when Lord David Cecil was also of the party.

Christine Longford, Julia and Violet Pakenham,
John Betjeman at Pakenham Hall, September 1930

Other guests included the second Earl of Birkenhead,
who was to introduce a collection of John's poems;
and Basil, Marquess of Dufferin and Ava, a brilliant
scholar at Balliol, who married Maureen Guinness
(above). John, who nicknamed Dufferin 'Little
Bloody' and spent holidays at his mansion,
Clandeboye, Co. Down, made his big eyes the
subject of a mock-Metaphysical poem. He was
devastated by Dufferin's death in the last year of the
Second World War, and wrote a moving threnody.

Castlepollard Show, 1925. Christine, her mother, and Edward

John also became a great friend of Frank Pakenham's elder brother, Edward, Earl of Longford, who had married Christine Trew in 1925. They invited him to their home, Pakenham Hall (now Tullynally), during the early 1930s. John painted a watercolour of the castle for the visitors' book in the style of the eighteenth-century artist Nicholas Pocock (page 131), and wrote underneath it:

Oh! Give me Pocock's pencil
   And give me Pocock's art!
And I will paint the Sylvan scenes
   Engraven on my heart!

'Mania' (John at Pakenham Hall, August 1930)

(*left to right*) Alastair Graham, Evelyn Waugh, Elizabeth Harman, John. Pakenham Hall, 1930

John as a priest, Pakenham, September 1930

Evelyn Waugh and Edward Longford

Fellow guests included Evelyn Waugh, Alastair Graham, Anthony Powell – who married Longford's sister Lady Violet Pakenham in 1934 – and the painter Henry Lamb, who had married another sister, Lady Pansy. Fancy dress charades and visits to Irish antiquities were among the entertainments. Evelyn Waugh wrote in his diary in August 1930, 'John B. became a bore rather with Irish peers and revivalist hymns and his enthusiasm for every sort of architecture.'

The wedding of Anthony Powell and Lady Violet Pakenham

Lady Pansy Lamb and her daughter Henrietta

Edward Longford and friends, Loch Derravaragh, August 1934

The Irish scene inspired John's early booklet of poems, *Sir John Piers*, published privately on the presses of *The Westmeath Examiner* under the pseudonym 'Epsilon' (now in *Collected Poems*).

I love your brown curls, | black in rain, my colleen,
*   I love your grey eyes, | by this verdant shore*
Two Derravaraghs | to plunge into and drown me,
*   Hold not those lakes of | light so near me more.*

THE ATTEMPT, Sir John Piers

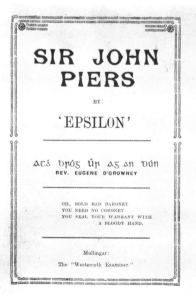

SIR JOHN
PIERS

BY

'EPSILON'

ᴀᴄᴀ́ ᴠᴘᴏ́ᵹ ᴜ́ᴘ ᴀᵹ ᴀɴ ᴠᴜ́ɴ
REV. EUGENE O'GROWNEY

OH, BOLD BAD BARONET
YOU NEED NO CORONET
YOU SEAL YOUR WARRANT WITH
   A BLOODY HAND.

Mullingar:
The "Westmeath Examiner."

Vol. 2   *Pl. 108*

TRISTERNAUGH ABBEY, Co.Westmeath, Pl.2.

Alongside his socialite life, John maintained his antiquarian and literary interests. He altered the title of his copy of *How to Look at Old Churches*, by H. Spencer Stowell MSA, Archaeological Recorder of the London Natural History Society, to *How Not To Look at Churches*, writing on the fly-leaf: 'An inaccurate, prejudiced and misleading book with wretched illustrations and a host of mistakes. An example of how not to write about churches.' He made sketches in parish churches and wrote to clergymen protesting against the proposed demolition of box pews. With Michael Dugdale and Lionel Perry he bicycled, in January 1930, to Olney, Bucks, to honour the memory of William Cowper who had written his Olney Hymns there.

Oh God the Olney Hymns abound
*   With words of Grace which Thou didst choose,*
And wet the elm above the hedge
*   Reflected in the winding Ouse.*

OLNEY HYMNS

The ruin in Co. Westmeath which moved John most was that of Tristernagh Abbey, where the last Sir John Piers, convicted of crim.con. in 1807, lived before his estates were sold. (John had read the romantic story in the library at Pakenham Hall.)

In the ivy dusty is the old lock rusty
*   That opens rasping on the place of graves,*
'Tis no home for mortals behind those portals
*   Where the shining dock grows and the nettle waves.*
Of the walls so ferny, near Tristernagh churchyard,
*   Often the learned historians write,*
And the Abbey splendificent, most magnificent,
*   Ribbed and springing in ancient night.*

TRISTERNAGH TO-DAY, Sir John Piers

John's upper-class contacts eventually brought him a job. His friend Maurice Hastings, who lived at Rousham House, Oxfordshire, gave him an introduction to his brother, H. de Cronin Hastings (right), editor of *The Architectural Review*. In 1930 John became an assistant editor of the magazine, to which he contributed several articles and book reviews and a few poems.

Through his work on the *Review*, he met some of the older generation of Arts and Crafts designers, such as C.F.A. Voysey, who wrote him postcards in bright blue ink in his fine hand, M.H. Baillie-Scott, whom John visited at his home in Kent, and George Walton, for whose family John helped to make provision after Walton died.

Telephone:
Victoria 6930.

Telegrams:
Buildable, Parl. London.

Mr J. Betjeman,
Assistant Editor.

The Architectural Review,
9 Queen Anne's Gate,
Westminster. S.W.1.

Many thanks for your letter. I envy you having to lunch with Baillie Scott. You must lunch with me as I can not write all I wish to reply to your letter. So I beg you to state the day on a post card; any day will suit me including Sunday.
C.F.A. Voysey. Sept. 23, 1936
73. Saint James S. S.W.1.

Pamela Mitford and her motor car in Ludgershall

John often stayed at Biddesden House, Andover, with his Oxford friend Bryan Guinness (now Lord Moyne), who married Diana Mitford in 1929. The house had been built for one of Marlborough's commanders, General Webb, who figures in Thackeray's *Henry Esmond*. A swag of military trophies decorated the front, and Webb's ghost was alleged to rampage round the house on a charger when a portrait of him was removed.

In a cottage belonging to Guinness lived Diana's sister Pamela Mitford (seen overleaf with Diana and her son Jonathan), who ran Guinness's farm for him. John, who was much attracted by her, called her 'Miss Pam', which was what the cowmen called her. She never took John's courtship very seriously, as she realised he was essentially 'metropolitan' while she was 'rural'. In 1936 she married the nuclear physicist Derek Jackson.

Nancy Mitford with Lord Alfred Douglas (*left*) and John at Brighton, *c.* 1930

A group at Biddesden, 1933. John (centre), cigarette drooping from lips, admires his trouser creases; with him (left to right), Ralf Jarvis, Heywood Hill (the bookseller, for whom Nancy later worked), Peter Ledesma, Jack Mitford.

Through Diana and Pamela he met the other Mitford sisters, including the Nazi sympathizer Unity (above left) and Nancy, to whom he wrote in 1932: 'If Pamela Mitford refuses me finally *you* might marry me – I'm rich, handsome and aristocratic.' Nancy made him a character in her 1931 novel *Christmas Pudding*.

John flying a kite at Biddesden in 1931;
and in more formal dress as he leaves for
The Architectural Review on Monday morning.

Marriage

It was through his work on *The Architectural Review* – the 'Archie Rev', as the printers and John and his friends called it – that he met his future wife, Penelope Chetwode. She had been sent along to see him by Robert Byron, who thought John might publish (as he did) an article by her on Indian temples. At their first meeting, John conducted a long telephone conversation with Pamela Mitford. But, Lady Betjeman recalls, 'We lay on the floor looking at photographs and began to fall in love.'

The photograph below was taken by L. Moholy-Nagy in 1933 shortly after their marriage.

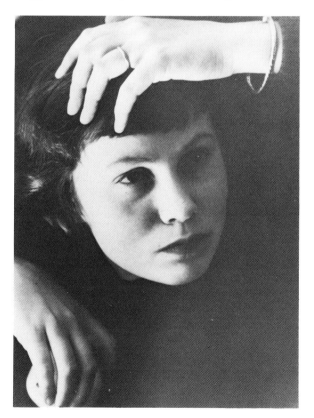

When she first met John, Penelope was a close friend of Johnnie Churchill the artist, a cousin of Randolph. Their mutual friend James Lees-Milne had once agreed to perform a pagan 'marriage' ceremony between them in a clearing of the woods of Wytham Abbey, Oxfordshire, where Johnnie's grandmother Lady Abingdon then lived. Johnnie and Penelope (dressed as ancient Greeks) set off to meet James, but muddled up the oak trees and were confronted instead by a suspicious gamekeeper.

James Lees-Milne

Penelope's father was Field-Marshal Lord Chetwode, a First World War hero who was now Commander-in-Chief in India. He and his formidable wife Hester ('Star') did not immediately welcome John, a scruffy and penniless poet, as a suitor for their daughter.

Johnnie Churchill

Mr. J. Carter   Captain W. E. Maxwell   Major D. C. Monro   Captain R. Lovett   Ris. Lal Singh   Captain R. Coates   K. B. Hafiz
Abdul Hakim

Mrs. Maxwell   Captain G. B. J. Kellie   The Hon'ble   H. E. the C-in-C   Lady Chetwode   Major R.F. Heyworth   Miss Chetwode
Mrs. Heyworth

They felt happier when she was with them in India, living the ceremonious life of a Raj Miss Sahib. Penelope formed a lasting attachment to India: in her seventies she is still leading treks through the foothills of the Himalayas in quest of Indian temples.

93

For a while, Penelope seemed determined to become a learned Indologist rather than get married; but she was not pleased when, during one of her absences in India, John transferred his attentions to her friend Wilhelmine Cresswell. 'I was furious and wrote and told him where to get off,' Lady Betjeman recalls. His semi-official engagement to 'Billa' was broken off and in 1938 she married (Sir) Roy Harrod. The Harrods remained among the Betjemans' best friends and took over their house at Uffington during the Second World War, when John was posted as British Press Attaché in Dublin.

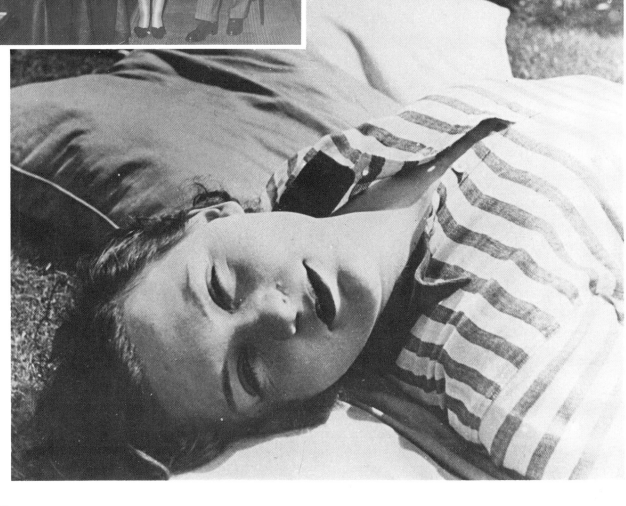

MOUNT ZION

OR

IN TOUCH WITH THE INFINITE

In 1931 John's first book of poems, *Mount Zion*, was published by Edward James. The binding was of firework paper from Brock's. Piles of copies were kept in the hallway of the Culross Street, London, house which John was then sharing with Randolph Churchill.

The best-known poem in the book has remained 'Death in Leamington', which has been described as 'Betjeman's "Lake Song of Innisfree"' –

She died in the upstairs bedroom
By the light of the ev'ning star
That shone through the plate-glass window
From over Leamington Spa.

DEATH IN LEAMINGTON

The Parade and Pump Room, Leamington Spa.
Watercolour by Ernest Haslehurst in George Morley's *Warwick and Leamington*, Blackie & Son, 1913

Mount Zion also contained 'The 'Varsity Students' Rag', which had first appeared in an Oxford undergraduate magazine. The Trocadero Restaurant (left) and the Criterion Restaurant, Piccadilly, were popular with undergraduates out on the razzle in London.

We had a rag at Monico's. We had a rag at the Troc.,
And the one we had at the Berkeley
> *gave the customers quite a shock.*
Then we went to the Popular, and after that – oh my!
I wish you'd seen the rag we had
> *in the Grill Room at the Cri.*

John's architectural essay *Ghastly Good Taste* was published by Chapman & Hall (of which Evelyn Waugh's father, Arthur, was a director) in 1933. At the back was a long fold-out illustration (part of which is shown here) by John's friend Peter Fleetwood-Hesketh, who in 1970 extended his drawing of the 'street of taste' into a nine-foot fold-out illustration for the reprint of the book by Anthony Blond.

Middle Class

1860. A Gothic Revival Church in the 'Early English' style influenced by Ruskin, but not so expensive.

1860. The Pimlico and South Kensington style, Palladio under the influence of Commercial success.

1865. The 'Mansard' style for large houses. Reaction in favour of the French.

1870. Queen Victoria's Own Classical style, suitable for station hotels and used in Victoria Street, London.

1880. Fire-station Holbeinesque style; executed in terra cotta and red brick.

Pamela Mitford held a party at Ludgershall, near Biddesden, in February 1934. John and Penelope, who had married clandestinely in 1933, were present, but the local paper listed them as 'Mr and Mrs Betzman' – probably because John's script 'j' looked like a script 'z'. Roy Harrod, a brilliant young economics don at Christ Church, Oxford, was also among the guests, with Unity Mitford and Bryan Guinness.

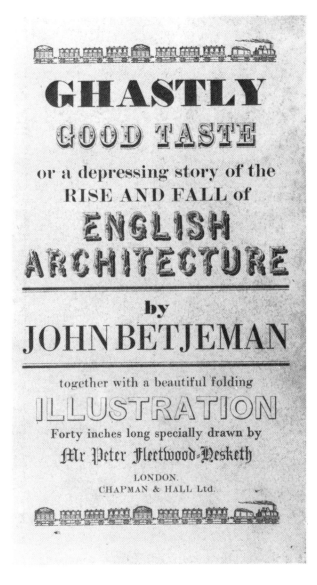

FEBRUARY 16, 1934

LUDGERSHALL.

ELKINS & SON, Central Garage and Sports Depot, Ludgershall. Established in 1915. Telephone 36. We undertake complete overhauls of all makes of cars—by competent mechanics—we recover hoods, we paint cars at moderate charges. Our motto is efficient service, moderate charges. Give us a trial, it will pay YOU. We supply Morris cars, Trojan and Ford products; come and consult us and get the best available terms. H.P. arranged if required.

DISTINGUISHED GUESTS AT SCOUTS HALL.— One of the jolliest events at the Scouts Hall for a long time was the party given by the Hon. Pamela Mitford, of Biddesden, on Saturday night, the attendance including the Rector of Ludgershall and the Vicar of Appleshaw, and other prominent residents in the two villages and district around. A picturesque figure was Miss Mitford's Hungarian maid, Frauline Rosa Szielbert, who was dressed in her national costume, and made the cakes which were provided as part of the refreshments. There were chipolatoes, too, and a host of other delicacies. Mr. Bob Bell acted as M.C., and his band played for dancing. He also provided a cabaret, the artists including Mr. F. Shadwell, the Hampshire Yokel comedian, and Miss Maud Clark. This proved very successful. Miss Mitford's own party included several distinguished guests, among its members being the Hon. Bryan Guinness, of Biddesden House; Miss Unity Mitford; Miss Volkoff; Mr. Volkoff; Mr. Christopher Bailey; Mr. Peter Ledesma; Mr. Willoughby; Mr. Kennedy; Mr. J. Kennedy; Mrs. Tomlin; Mr. and Mrs. Betzman; and Mr. Roy Harrod. There were nearly 200 present altogether.

Uffington

After living for a while in somewhat squalid London flats, John and Penelope moved, in 1934, into a farmhouse at Uffington, Berkshire, in the Vale of the White Horse.

John became a churchwarden at St Mary's Church, Uffington. In 1937 he paid for the cleaning of the Royal arms.

Tonight we feel the muffled peal
  Hang on the village like a pall;
It overwhelms the towering elms –
  That death-reminding dying fall;
The very sky no longer high
  Comes down within the reach of all.
Imprisoned in a cage of sound
Even the trivial seems profound.

UFFINGTON

The Betjemans were rich enough to afford a German maid, Paula Steinbrecher, seen here in 1935.

. . . after Sunday supper [Penelope] would play the piano and lead hymns with a fine *bel canto*, while the rest joined in . . . When the German maid, Paula, burst in to clear the remains of the meal, Penelope would dismiss her abruptly, '*Aber, Paula, Sie können nicht einkommen. Wir haben Gottesdienst.*' ('Paula, you can't come in. We are having a religious service.')
    Sir Maurice Bowra, *Memories 1898–1939* (Weidenfeld & Nicolson, London 1966)

Penelope kept her white Arab mare Moti, a present from her father, in the stables; she also had a goat, Snowdrop, which provided the household with milk.

Evening Standard
(EVENING STANDARD CO. LTD.)

47, SHOE LANE,
LONDON, E.C.4.

January 15, 1934.

PERSONAL.

John Betjemann, Esq.,
"The Architectural Review,"
9, Queen Anne's Gate,
S.W.1.

Dear Mr. Betjemann,

This is to confirm the arrangement
we made in our recent conversation -
that you will join the editorial staff
of the "Evening Standard" on January 29,
at a salary of sixteen guineas per week,
for a definite period of six months, the
engagement to be terminable thereafter
by six months' notice by either party.

It is a condition of your
engagement that you shall do no
journalistic work for any other periodical,
except by special arrangement with this
firm. I shall, of course, always be ready to consider any
reasonable request of this nature.

Yours faithfully,

Percy Cudlipp
EDITOR.

In January 1934 John was appointed film critic of the
Evening Standard. He had caught Lord Beaverbrook's
eye in December 1933 with an article on 'Peers
Without Tears'. His salary was 16gns a week: at that
time, over £800 a year was a high wage for a man of
twenty-seven.

Osbert Lancaster recalls that John was given the
sack for writing a merciless critique of an actress who
was the girlfriend of a big movie mogul. But the
paper's advertisers complained so much at John's
disappearance that he had to be re-employed at a
higher salary.

Each day he took the train to London from Challow
station. (He made this drawing of old cottages, now
demolished, at West Challow.) On the train he took
notes on the dialogues of his fellow-passengers, such
as one old lady who confided that she was very partial
to 'dye-gestive biscuits'.

The Uffington visitors' book for 1934–6 is full of
famous names: Evelyn Waugh (left) came down;
Cyril Connolly (below); Noël Blakiston (later head of
the Public Record Office) with his wife Georgiana
(Giana); Peter Quennell and his future wife Marcelle
Rothe, seen here in a clinch with John.

Among the Betjemans' neighbours was the eccentric Lord Berners (below), who lived in the Georgian mansion Faringdon Hall with his friend Robert Heber-Percy. The Betjemans were frequent dinner guests at Faringdon – on one occasion with H.G. Wells and Moura Budberg (known as 'Countess Bedbug'). Berners was a talented composer, admired by Stravinsky, and a patron of the arts; but he also enjoyed the schoolboy humour which appealed to John, such as playing a tune on the grand piano with his bottom. He built a folly, a tall and purposeless tower, at Faringdon, on which John wrote an unpublished poem.

A village concert at Uffington, 1935 with Lord Berners at piano, Osbert Lancaster on flute, Penelope Betjeman at table, Maurice Bowra, John Betjeman, Cara Lancaster and Adrian Bishop singing; recorded by Osbert Lancaster.

Penelope was all for a quiet country life, but John still enjoyed flirting with High Society, making occasional appearances in *The Tatler*, *The Bystander* or *The Sketch*, which on 21 November 1934 showed John ('who is definitely one of the intelligentsia') driving with Peter Quennell and Marcelle Rothe in Penelope's phaeton, and showing his teddy-bear Archie to Lady Mary Pakenham. Lady Mary took the two portraits of John, which she captioned 'Charm' and 'The great man in his study'.

1. MRS. JOHN BETJEMAN is taking MR. PETER QUENNELL, the distinguished poet, and MISS MARCELLE ROTHE out for a drive in her old-world phaeton, drawn by her white Arab, Moti. She was Miss Penelope Chetwode.

2. VISCOUNTESS HASTINGS is here posed with a charming little kitten. She was Miss Cristina Casati, and is the wife of the Earl of Huntingdon's heir.

3. MR. JOHN BETJEMAN, who is definitely one of the Intelligentsia, is the author of " Ghastly Good Taste " and other books. He owns a Teddy bear, " Archie," which he is showing to LADY MARY PAKENHAM.

4. MRS. JOHN BETJEMAN is posed with her white Arab, Moti. Her father, Field-Marshal Sir Philip Chetwode, is the Commander-in-Chief of the Army in India.

Moti, Penelope's beautiful white Arab, took up much
of her time. Lord Berners painted a picture of her
riding Moti, from a Gaumont British film still of 1935.
He allowed the horse into Faringdon House, and
painted another portrait of Penelope standing beside
Moti in the great hall.

Visitors to Uffington and Faringdon were usually
conscripted for a ride in Penelope's phaeton.
Even John, who was far from enthusiastic about
horses, enjoyed the Regency experience, taking a
mandarin-like pose in the back of the trap with a
raised umbrella.

Penelope Betjeman, H.G. Wells, Moura Budberg, Robert
Heber-Percy, and Lord Berners

Lady Alexandra Haig, Penelope Betjeman, Robert Heber-Percy,
Aldous Huxley, and Lord Berners at Faringdon House

Four of John's caricatures of Penelope, from '5 Incidents in My Life':

Asking Lord Bath to give her the recipe
for stuffed eggs

Gorging herself with butter *and* marmalade
on a religious retreat

Asking the late Queen Mary,
'Do you know the work of Gropius, Ma'am?'

Revealing to a sceptical old gentleman out hunting that she is the daughter
of the Commander-in-Chief in India

Another Uffington neighbour was Samuel Gurney, who lived at Compton Beauchamp. Although of the famous Quaker family, he was a High Anglican. John and Penelope were very fond of him. Penelope is seen here at one of his lavish picnics, in 1935, giving children a ride on Moti.

Frank ('Adrian') Bishop came to live near the Betjemans in an Uffington farmhouse in 1935, to recover from an attack of *Encephalitis lethargica* (sleepy sickness). He originally came from Dublin, where his father was maltster in Jameson's distillery. 'He was used to dominating any group in which he mixed,' Maurice Bowra wrote, 'and in this, as in other ways, he resembled Oscar Wilde, who came from the same layer of Dublin society. . . . Everyone became more responsive and more agreeable when his genius turned their most casual remarks into fantastic and fanciful shapes.' At Uffington, he was an important figure in John's and Penelope's lives. Through the influence of their confessor, Father Harton, Rector of Baulking, he entered the Anglican monastery of Nashdom Abbey, near Taplow. He was killed in a fall in a Tehran hotel in 1942. It was rumoured that he had been working for British Intelligence.

In September 1935 John went down to Hove with Bishop and Michael Dugdale to visit Lord Alfred Douglas – 'A very horrible old man,' Dugdale later recorded in his diary. Dugdale took the photograph of Bishop (right), and this one of John, on Brighton beach.

Lord Alfred Douglas visited Uffington in the same year. Wilfrid Blunt, whose brother Christopher and his wife were also living in Uffington at that time, recalls

a memorable occasion when Adrian [Bishop], Penelope Betjeman and Lord Alfred Douglas joined us to judge the local baby show. Owing to some confusion over the numbering of the babies the prize did not go, as had been intended, to the deserving infant of the local milkman, and for many weeks afterwards milk was very hard to come by. Penelope had ridden over, and while the judging was in progress her horse had seized the opportunity to roll in a dungheap. Lord Alfred and I were therefore ordered to scrub the animal down.

Wilfrid Blunt, MARRIED TO A SINGLE LIFE, Michael Russell, London 1983

John Sutro is Tom, man-of-all-work at " The Sailor's Return."

Vivien Braun is camera director

"The Sailor's Return"

The Film with a Mayfair Cast

Lady Caroline Paget is Tulip, Princess of Dahomey, the sailor's wife

DAVID GARNETT'S story, *The Sailor's Return*, provides the scenario for the John Sutro - Cecil Beaton film that's being made at Ashcombe, Cecil Beaton's house in Dorset. Cecil Beaton is the sailor hero who arrives home to be a pub-keeper, with a Princess of Dahomey (Lady Caroline Paget) as his wife, and a child called Sambo. The village doesn't take kindly to them, and a storm of jealousy, snobbery, and religious complications ends in the sailor's murder. John Sutro, the villain of the piece, is a director of London Films, but an amateur actor, and so is John Betjeman, who is the *Evening Standard* film expert. The only professionals are Vivien Braun and Guy Branch, who are directing the production

Left : Cecil Beaton is William Targett, the sailor ; he dies in agony with a pitch-fork through his back

Left : John Betjeman is the clergyman

John's and Evelyn Waugh's Oxford friend John Sutro (page 56) had become a film-maker. In 1935 he put up the money for a film, *The Sailor's Return*, which was made at Cecil Beaton's home, Ashcombe in Dorset. *The Bystander* called it 'The Film with a Mayfair Cast.' Cecil Beaton was the sailor (below), Lady Caroline Paget played his wife Tulip, Princess Dahomey, and John took the part of a clergyman. Sutro himself played Tom, a man-of-all-work.

'A plain Publicity Manager.' Portrait of Jack Beddington by Rex Whistler

William Scudamore Mitchell

During the 1930s, John began working for Jack Beddington, publicity director of Shell – first as a freelance, then as a staff member. It was Beddington who recruited well-known artists such as John Piper, Graham Sutherland and E. McKnight Kauffer to design posters for Shell; he also appointed John editor of a series of English county guides, which began appearing in 1933.

John always called Beddington 'Beddioleman' because an American named Grimaldi, on leaving the director's office, had said: 'Well, hi, Beddy, ol' man!' From 1936 John's closest colleague at Shell-Mex House was William Scudamore Mitchell, known as 'Scudamore'. Together they used to compose indecent and wholly libellous limericks about Beddington's secretary. John also sent Mitchell this rhyme on a postcard:

'Ere church bell panged on Hintock Green,
Full many a curious thing he did:
He sprinkled his hair with Beddioline
And went for a walk with a caryatid.

William Mitchell explained: 'We were searching for a name for a new kind of motor oil; and John suggested it should be "Beddioline" – after Beddioleman, of course.'

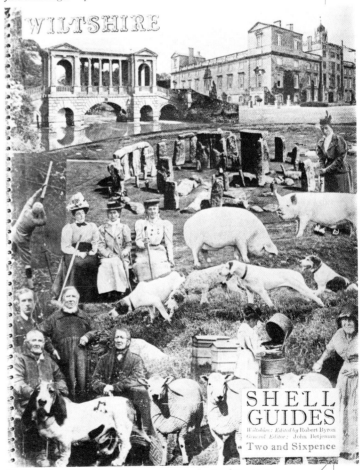

Shell Guide to Wiltshire, 1935; cover design by Lord Berners

John gave William Scudamore Mitchell the original manuscripts of two of his poems, 'Love in a Valley' and 'Holy Trinity, Sloane Street'. The former appeared in *Continual Dew* (Murray, 1937) for which E. McKnight Kauffer designed a surrealist jacket; the latter, in *Old Lights for New Chancels* (1941).

   Continual Dew also contained John's poem 'The Arrest of Oscar Wilde at the Cadogan Hotel', which had first appeared in June 1933 in the magazine *Oxford and Cambridge*, of which Randolph Churchill was a sub-editor (see page 68).

He sipped at a weak hock and seltzer
   As he gazed at the London skies
Through the Nottingham lace of the curtains
   Or was it his bees-winged eyes? . . .

'More hock, Robbie – where is the seltzer?
   Dear boy, pull again at the bell!
They are all little better than cretins,
   Though this is the Cadogan Hotel.' . . .

CONTINUAL
DEW
BY JOHN BETJEMAN

The death of King George V in 1936 moved John to a poem which also appeared in *Continual Dew*.

The big blue eyes are shut which saw wrong clothing
   And favourite fields and coverts from a horse;
Old men in country houses hear clocks ticking
   Over thick carpets with a deadened force . . .

DEATH OF KING GEORGE V

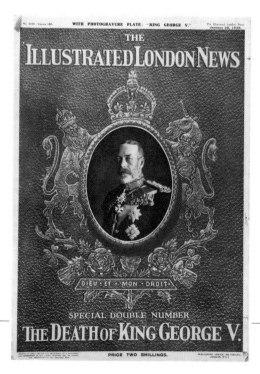

[Handwritten manuscript of 'In Holy Trinity, Sloane Street']

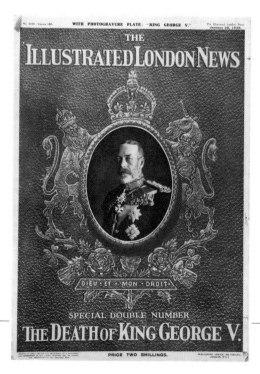

In September 1935, Penelope attended a conference of Orientalists in Rome. John wrote her a series of facetious letters in the mock-Irish dialect they affected in correspondence. His usual nickname for her was 'Propeller', but the letters are variously addressed to 'My darling enveloppee . . . developpee . . . pequilloeppee . . . Pemellowppee . . . Utrilloppee . . . Udolloppee . . . Pedrilloppee . . . Peegrilluppee . . . and Caterpillarpee'.

In 1936 Penelope and John visited the exotic artist Stephen Tennant in his house at Wilsford in the Avon valley. A fellow guest was Arthur Waley, the translator of Chinese poetry.

Stephen Tennant

John and Penelope's first child, Paul, was born in 1938. Penelope put him on the back of a horse before he could walk. John was more concerned to introduce him to the pleasures of travel by train.

Arthur Waley

112

John, who was to be a major 'television personality' from the 1950s to the 1980s, was already making television programmes in the 1930s. Here he is taking part in a 'Tactile Bee' at the Alexandra Palace studios in 1938, with Andrew Miller Jones (scorer) and Christopher Stone (Master of Ceremonies). The object of the game was to identify things from their feel.

John's new book of poems of 1940, *Old Lights for New Chancels*, contained his verses on Captain Webb, the cross-channel swimmer. They are meant to be read with a Lancashire accent.

The gas was on in the Institute,
  The fire was up in the gym,
A man was running a mineral line,
  A lass was singing a hymn,
When Captain Webb the Dawley man,
  Captain Webb from Dawley,
Came swimming along the old canal
That carried the bricks to Lawley.

  A SHROPSHIRE LAD .

At the outbreak of the Second World War in 1939, several of John's friends joined the armed forces. John Sparrow became a colonel in the Coldstream Guards. John himself volunteered for the Royal Air Force but was turned down after failing a psychology test which showed that he was terrified of spiders. Eventually Sir Kenneth Clark (above right), a friend from Maurice Bowra's Oxford *salon*, found him a post in the Films Division of the Ministry of Information.

CAPTAIN WEBB'S EXPLOIT.
THIS ENGLISHMAN SWAM ACROSS THE ENGLISH CHANNEL FROM DOVER TO CALAIS ON AUGUST 25TH 1875. — THE ONLY MAN IN THE WORLD EVER KNOWN WHO PERFORMED SUCH A FEAT. — TIME 21¾ HOURS.

Wartime Ireland and London

John with children in the dining room of Collinstown Park

Left to right: Paul Betjeman, Dr Kissan, Principal of Maynooth College, Dublin, Sir John Maffey and John Betjeman

In 1941 John was posted to Dublin as Press Attaché to Sir John Maffey, the British Representative. He and Penelope were lent a Georgian mansion called Collinstown near Dublin airport – the first place the Germans would have overrun if they had invaded. John got on well with Maffey, an impressive proconsular figure who had been Governor of the Sudan. John's reports were read with pleasure in Whitehall; but at first he was widely regarded by the Irish as a British spy. One IRA soldier was deputed to assassinate him. Luckily John was away on mission at the time; and when the IRA later read his poems, they concluded he could not possibly be a spy. After the Japanese attack on Pearl Harbor in 1941, Penelope was told she must no longer go riding with the Japanese ambassador.

In Ireland the Betjemans made friends with Emily, Lady Hemphill, an American heiress and brilliant horsewoman who lived at Tulira Castle in the heart of the Yeats country at Ardrahan, Co. Galway. John was entranced by the Victorian house, which had been built round a fifteenth-century tower in 1882 by George Ashlin for Edward Martyn, a leading figure in the Celtic Revival. The staircase, stained glass and other decorations were executed in 1891 by John Dibblee Crace.

Penelope Betjeman recalls that Emily Hemphill was the only woman of whom she was ever jealous. She went to bed one night, leaving John and Lady Hemphill talking, and was tortured by fears that they were having an affair. 'But I needn't have worried, as she was already wildly in love with a man called Ion Villiers-Stuart, whom she later married.'

John's poem 'Ireland with Emily' described a bicycle ride he made with Lady Hemphill, and when the poem was printed in *New Bats in Old Belfries* (1945), he inscribed a copy to her.

Has it held, the warm June weather?
  Draining shallow sea-pools dry,
When we bicycled together
  Down the bohreens fuchsia-high.

IRELAND WITH EMILY

Both Penelope and John became friends of Father Paddy Brown, a professor at the Roman Catholic college of Maynooth. This photograph shows John and Paul taking a dip while staying with Professor Brown.

Bust of Emily, Lady Hemphill, by Brenda Gogarty, daughter of Oliver St John Gogarty

Part of John's duties as Press Attaché was to make arrangements for, and entertain, distinguished visitors to Ireland. One was Laurence Olivier, who came over to make the film of *Henry V* because, unlike England, Ireland still had an abundance of young men to be extras, and horses for them to ride. The Battle of Agincourt was filmed on Lord Powerscourt's demesne at Enniskerry, Co. Wicklow.

Another film star visitor was Leslie Howard. Beverley Nichols came over but found the Betjemans' house too dank and mossy to stay in, and moved into a hotel. Professor C.M. Joad, a star of 'The Brains Trust' famous for his opening gambit 'It depends what you mean by . . .' also came to stay and was introduced to riding.

At the end of John's service as Press Attaché, President de Valéra gave him this signed photograph.

John learnt the Irish language, spent much time talking to Irish people in pubs and was a highly popular figure. When he left Dublin in 1943, his departure was front page news in *The Irish Times*.

> He . . . looked upon it as his duty not only to interpret England to the Irish, but also to interpret Ireland sympathetically to the English, and if any English Pressman or visitor went away with an unsympathetic view of Ireland it was not the fault of Mr Betjeman. . . .

THE IRISH TIMES, 14 June 1943

Doctor G. and Mrs. Hunter Dunn
request the pleasure of
the company of

Mr. and Mrs. John Betjeman

at the marriage of his daughter

Joan Hunter,
with
Mr. H. Wycliffe Jackson,

at St. Mark's Church, Farnborough, Hants.,
on Saturday, January 20th, 1945,
at 2 o'clock,

and afterwards at
The Red House,
Reading Road,
Farnborough, Hants.   R.S.V.P.

John returned to the Ministry of Information where, in the canteen, he met an attractive girl from Aldershot called Joan Hunter Dunn. She was the inspiration of his poem 'A Subaltern's Love-song', which was first published in the magazine *Horizon*, edited by Cyril Connolly, in February 1941. He was invited to her wedding in 1945 but was unable to attend.

Miss J. Hunter Dunn, Miss J. Hunter Dunn,
Furnish'd and burnish'd by Aldershot sun,
What strenuous singles we played after tea,
We in the tournament – you against me!

A Subaltern's Love-song

John did not make such a hit with Colonel Norman Scorgie, who came to the Ministry of Information from the Stationery Office and pinned up notices exhorting the staff to 'pull their weight'. Soon after Scorgie's arrival, John entered a crowded lift in which he recognized Scorgie. Turning to the lift man, he inquired 'Have you met this Colonel *Scroggie*? I hear he's not really *pulling his weight.*' Scorgie summoned Sir Kenneth Clark and told him: 'This man Betjeman is half-baked. We must get rid of him.' But Clark replied: 'Betjeman has one idea a month which is better than anybody else's all year,' and John was reprieved.

In 1944 John was posted to the Admiralty, Bath, where the present Lord Weinstock was his junior.

In 1943 John, who had made regular appearances on 'The Brains Trust', became one of the new question-masters. He presided for the first time at the session broadcast on 28 September in the BBC Home Service and 3 October in the Forces Programme.

Joan Hunter Dunn

Farnborough

In 1945 the Betjeman family moved into a late seventeenth-century house, formerly the Rectory, at Farnborough, Berkshire (page 131). Their daughter, Candida, had been born in Dublin in 1942. Bassano took this sun-dappled group in the garden.

> Father has bought us a beautiful William and Mary House 700 feet up on the downs above Wantage, with 12 acres of land, including a wood and two fields. It is a dream of beauty but has no water and no light and is falling down and needs six servants so it will probably kill us in the end.

(Penelope Betjeman to Wilhelmine Harrod, 9 July 1945)

FARNBOROUGH WOMEN'S INSTITUTE.

In 1945 John had to have a minor operation at the Acland Hospital, Oxford, for a sebacious cyst on his stomach. He was nursed by Mary Renault, the novelist, who remembered his looking down from the hospital window at a girls' school playground and telling her they were 'just like Ronald Searle's St Trinian's'. After the operation he went to Beaulieu, Hampshire, for two weeks to convalesce. There he met Clemency, daughter of General Buckland, who figures in one of his most atmospheric poems, 'Youth and Age on Beaulieu River, Hants.'

> *Early sun on Beaulieu water*
> *Lights the undersides of oaks,*
> *Clumps of leaves it floods and blanches,*
> *All transparent glow the branches*
> *Which the double sunlight soaks;*
> *To her craft on Beaulieu water*
> *Clemency the General's daughter*
> *Pulls across with even strokes.*

By the late 1940s (this Osbert Lancaster cartoon of him appeared in *The Sketch* of 3 March 1948) John's eccentricities were becoming public property: the baggy trousers, shapeless hats and championing of despised Victorian architecture.

"*Mr. John Betjeman awaiting inspiration and the 4.47 from Didcot.*"

I am the very model of a perfect Betjemanian,
I know all the London churches,
> *from R.C. to Sandemanian,*
I know that neo-Gothick is the only truly cultural
And my appetite for Butterfield is positively vultural.
I've a suitable derision for folk-weave and for pottery
And a corresponding passion both for
> *Streetery and Scottery.*
I bore my simpler friends with talk of
> *Voysey and of Mackintosh –*
If I can't remember details you can
> *count on me to pack in tosh.*
I cultivate the hideous, my room is aspidistrical,
I poke fun at archaeologists and all matters
> *Wykehamistical . . .*

AN ALTERNATIVE SONG FOR 'THE PIRATES OF PENZANCE', by John ['the Widow'] Lloyd

The Betjeman children were becoming proficient in pony-riding. A series of gymkhanas and hunter trials gave John the idea for one of his funniest poems.

It's awf'lly bad luck on Diana,
  Her ponies have swallowed their bits;
She fished down their throats with a spanner
  And frightened them all into fits . . .

HUNTER TRIALS

In 1948, John contributed the introduction to *The Eighteen Nineties*, an anthology of period verse and prose published by his friend Martin Secker. Among the 'nineties figures who interested John most were Theo Marzials, Max Beerbohm (above), who wrote to him in 1949 about the publisher Leonard Smithers (right), and Theodore Wratislaw, who figures in John's poem 'On Seeing an Old Poet in the Café Royal':

'Where is Oscar? Where is Bosie?
  Have I seen that man before?
And the old one in the corner,
  Is it really Wratislaw?'
Scent of Tutti-Frutti-Sen-Sen
  And cheroots upon the floor.

Theodore Wratislaw

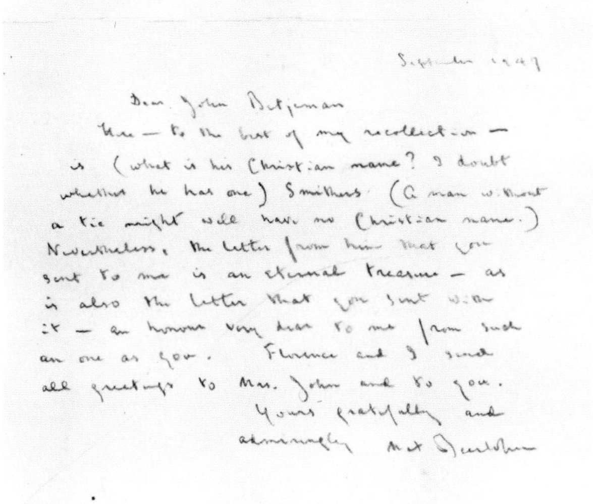

September 1947

Dear John Betjeman
Here — to the best of my recollection — is (what is his Christian name? I doubt whether he has one) Smithers. (A man without a tie might well have no Christian name.) Nevertheless, the letter from him that you sent to me is an eternal treasure — as is also the letter that you sent with it — an honour very dear to me from such an one as you. Florence and I send all greetings to Mrs. John and to you.
Yours gratefully and admiringly Max Beerbohm

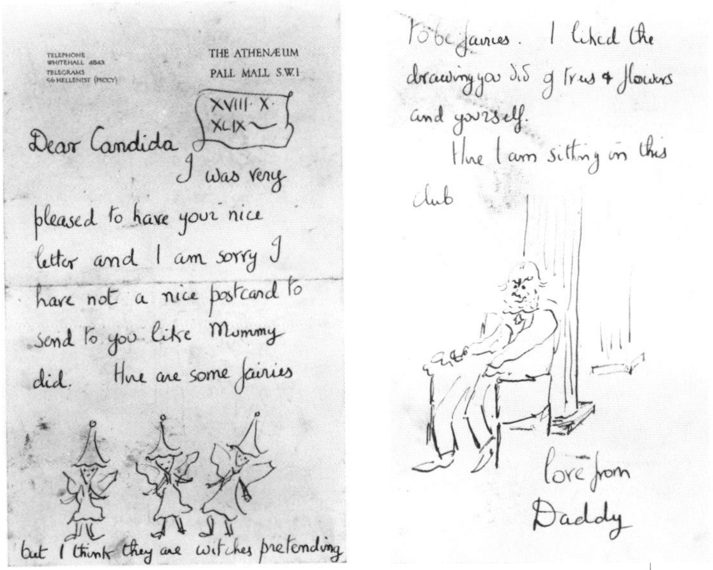

TELEPHONE WHITEHALL 4843
TELEGRAMS HELLENIST (PICCY)

THE ATHENÆUM
PALL MALL S.W.1

XVIII. X.
XLIX

Dear Candida
I was very pleased to have your nice letter and I am sorry I have not a nice postcard to send to you like Mommy did. Here are some fairies

but I think they are witches pretending

To be fairies. I liked the drawing you did of trees & flowers and yourself.
Here I am sitting in this club

love from
Daddy

When away from his children, in London, John wrote them comic illustrated letters. This example, of 1949, ends with a self-portrait in The Athenaeum.

The last London tram finished its run on the night of 5 July 1952. A message in international code-flags at a flag manufacturer's in the Old Kent Road read 'Breakers ahead of you – Good-bye' – a last salute to the London County Council trams. It was a sad day for John, who celebrated trams, both horse-drawn and electric, in several of his poems.

On roaring iron down the Holloway Road
  The red trams and the brown trams pour,
And little each yellow-faced jolting load
  Knows of the fast-shut grained oak door.

THE SANDEMANIAN MEETING-HOUSE IN HIGHBURY QUADRANT

Eve Disher, the girlfriend of John's Marlborough friend Sir Arthur Elton, painted this portrait of John in 1951. He thought it made him look like the actor Alastair Sim. The photograph shows John at about the same date.

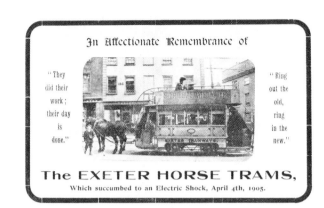

John reviewed books for *Time and Tide*, and became literary editor. But in December 1953 the magazine's autocratic owner, Lady Rhondda, took him to the Caprice Restaurant and told him he was fired.
In mild retaliation, John wrote his poem 'Caprice':

I sat only two tables off from the one I was sacked at,
    Just three years ago,
And here was another meringue like the one
      which I hacked at,
    When pride was brought low
And the coffee arrived – the place which she
      had to use tact at
    For striking a blow.

'I'm making some changes next week
      in the organisation
    And though I admire
Your work for me, John, yet the need
      to increase circulation
    Means you must retire:
An outlook more global than yours is the qualification
    I really require.' . . .

Caprice

Wantage

In 1951 the Betjemans moved from Farnborough to The Mead, a Victorian house in nearby Wantage. Their friend Douglas Woodruff, editor of the Roman Catholic magazine *The Tablet* and an authority on King Alfred the Great, thought it likely the house stood on the site of Alfred's palace.

John at Wantage station with 1857 locomotive

*Richard Wood
Contract p. 8*

WANTAGE AND GROVE,

BERKS.

Particulars and Conditions of Sale

OF THE VALUABLE

LEASEHOLD

ESTATE,
"The Mead,"

FREEHOLD ACCOMMODATION

MEADOW & ARABLE

LAND,

COTTAGES AND GARDENS,

WHICH

J. & E. BELCHER

Are favoured with instructions,

TO SELL BY AUCTION,

AT THE "BEAR" HOTEL, WANTAGE,

On Wednesday, July 19th, 1871,

AT 3 FOR 4 O'CLOCK IN THE AFTERNOON,

IN LOTS.

L. JOTCHAM, *Solicitor, Wantage.*

J. Lewis & Co., Printers, &c., Wantage.

John at The Mead

The Mead Waterfowl Farm
Wantage Berkshire

Tel. Wantage 150   Station: Wantage Road

The Hon. Mrs Betjeman

Specialist in Table Breeds of Ducks and Geese

PRICE LIST - DUCKS - MARCH/APRIL 1954

AYLESBURY (Weston's World-Famous Strain). The only indigenous
English Breed. Poor Layer but quickest grower among table ducks.
Averages 6 lbs at 9-10 wks.
          Day-olds 42/- dozen. Stock Birds Two Guineas each.

PEKIN (Johnson's Giant White Strain). Native of China and first
imported to England about 70 years ago. White with orange bill.
Lays more eggs than the Aylesbury but does not grow quite so
quickly. Averages 5½ lbs at 9-10 wks.
          Day-olds 42/- dozen. Stock Birds Two Guineas each.

PEKIN X AYLESBURY The finest Table Cross. Top weight on this farm
1953 was reached with one of these birds : 7lbs 4oz at 10 weeks.
          Day-olds 42/- dozen.

SILVER APPLEYARD A triple-purpose breed evolved by England's
premier duck expert, Mr. Reginald Appleyard. For beauty of plumage
it can hold its own with most of the ornamentals. Lays more eggs
than either of the above breeds with high fertility rate. Averages
5 lbs at 9 weeks.
          Day-olds 36/- dozen. Stock Birds Two Guineas each.

BLACK EAST INDIAN A beautiful ornamental Variety (though surplus
birds make delicious eating!) Small, black plumage with a marvellous
beetle green sheen.
          Mated Pair Three Guineas.

G E E S E

ROMAN A small white Italian goose (very likely descended from the
geese which gave warning on the Capitol when Rome was beseiged by
the Gauls in 365 B.C.) This breed is becoming increasingly popular
in England because the Roman matures quickly and fits nicely into a
small oven, averaging 12 lbs at four to five months. Lays consider-
ably more eggs than a goose of the heavier breeds. DIFFICULT TO
SUPPLY PRESENT DEMAND so BOOK EARLY to avoid disappointment.
3 wks (off heat) 18/6 each. 6 wks 30/-. Stock Birds: Geese 4 gns.
Ganders 5 guineas.
                                              P.T.O.

To make some much-needed money, Penelope opened The Mead Waterfowl Farm (Reynolds Stone executed the wood engraving for the letter-head) and King Alfred's Kitchen, of which John was a director, a tea-shop serving home-made cakes and preserves. The Kitchen, which was formally blessed by Father (later Bishop) Trevor Huddleston, author of *Naught for Your Comfort*, became a popular meeting place for Oxford undergraduates with motor cars.

A MONK IN KING ALFRED'S TOWN

When the Rev. Fr. Trevor Huddleston was in Wantage last week, he blessed "King Alfred's Kitchen," a new restaurant in the town. Mr. John Betjeman is a director of the restaurant. The Superior of the Community (Fr. Raynes) and the Vicar of Wantage (the Rev. A. Chetwynd Talbot) are also seen in the picture

As a treat for the local children (and some of their parents) John would perform Vachel Lindsay's bombastic poem 'The Congo', beating out its savage rhythms with a stick on a saucepan lid. (Years earlier, at Heddon Court school, he had got the boys to chant and thump the poem in unison, with the result that his classroom had to be moved well away from all the others.)

Fat black bucks in a wine-barrel room,
Barrel-house kings, with feet unstable,
Sagged and reeled and pounded on the table,
Pounded on the table,
Beat an empty barrel with the handle of a broom,
Hard as they were able,
Boom, boom, BOOM. . . .

    Vachel Lindsay, THE CONGO

In 1954 John Murray published a new book of poems by John, *A Few Late Chrysanthemums*. It contained his poem 'How to Get On in Society'. *Time and Tide* had held a competition to write a poem with that title in John's manner: 'I didn't dare to enter, in case I lost,' he said. John's poem, which was also printed as a pendant to Nancy Mitford's *Noblesse Oblige*, incorporated all the phrases which 'U' people were not supposed to use. It begins 'Phone for the fish-knives, Norman . . .' and ends:

Beg pardon, I'm soiling the doileys
  With afternoon tea-cakes and scones.

A Few Late Chrysanthemums also contained 'Verses turned in aid of a Public Subscription (1952) towards the restoration of the Church of St Katherine Chiselhampton, Oxon', which had been first published as a pamphlet with an illustration of the little classical-style church of 1762, by John's friend Sir Henry Rushbury RA. The building had been dismissed by *Murray's Handbook* of 1894 as 'a modern church with a bell-turret such as is usually placed on stables'.

St. Katherine's Church

Chiſelhampton, Oxfordſhire

John Piper was first introduced to John in 1937. He and his wife Myfanwy (*née* Evans) became great friends of the Betjemans. The two Johns were associated in the Shell Guides. The Pipers lived in a farmhouse near Henley-on-Thames. While staying with them there in the war, John Betjeman helped to hand-colour Piper's *Brighton Aquatints*. Myfanwy was the inspiration of two Betjeman poems.

Pink May, double may, dead laburnum,
  Shedding an Anglo-Jackson shade,
Shall we ever, my staunch Myfanwy,
  Bicycle down to North Parade?
Kant on the handle-bars, Marx in the saddlebag,
  Light my touch on your shoulder-blade.

Myfanwy at Oxford

John Betjeman, Lady David Cecil, Lord David Cecil, Penelope and Candida Betjeman at Henley-on-Thames, early 1950s

John Piper and Penelope Betjeman at Henley-on-Thames, early 1950s

John Betjeman and John Piper

John's sketch of Pakenham Hall (now Tullynally)

John's watercolour of the Old Rectory, Farnborough, near Wantage

John wrote 'Lord Cozens Hardy' in December 1955
after visiting Letheringsett Hall, near Holt, Norfolk,
with Roy and Wilhelmine Harrod, who lived at Holt.
Lord Cozens-Hardy had been a divorce court judge in
the late nineteenth century. When the poem was
published in *The Saturday Book* of 1956, John altered
the name to 'Lord Barton Bendish' so as not to give
offence to the Cozens-Hardy family. The poem was
accompanied by an illustration of the mausoleum by
John Piper.

Oh Lord Cozens Hardy
    Your mausoleum is cold,
The dry brown grass is brittle
    And frozen hard the mould
And where those Grecian columns rise
    So white among the dark
Of yew trees and of hollies in
    That corner of the park
By Norfolk oaks surrounded
    Whose branches seem to talk,
I know, Lord Cozens Hardy,
    I would not like to walk.

Cloth Fair and Radnor Walk

In the mid 1950s John, whose main income now came from book reviewing, broadcasting and his poems, began dividing his time between Wantage and a house in Cloth Fair in the City of London.

This was the nicest place in London to live in because everything could be reached on foot, down alleys and passages. Like all county towns it had a bit of every trade. I was lucky enough to live in Cloth Fair where there was still a shop which sold cloth. On some weekly nights there was bell-ringing from the tower of St Bartholomew's the Great, just such bells as the walled city must have heard when there were 106 churches in its square mile. Behind me was Smithfield meat market with its cheerful, Chaucerian characters and medieval-looking hand barrows.

John Betjeman, OBSERVER colour magazine, 24 July 1977

Edensor, near Chatsworth (home of the Dukes of Devonshire), where John often stayed, drawn by Osbert Lancaster.

Princess Margaret was a fan of John's poetry.
John and Penelope attended her wedding to Anthony
Armstrong-Jones (Lord Snowdon) in 1960.

Two new friends were the novelist Kingsley Amis
(above right; John first met him in 1958), one of the
so-called 'Angry Young Men' of the 1950s, and
Gilbert Harding (right) whom he met through his
growing television work. With Compton Mackenzie,
Malcolm Muggeridge and Sir Mortimer Wheeler,
John and Harding were among the earliest 'television
personalities'.

John was also becoming well-known in the 1950s as a formidable conservationist of architecture, including street architecture such as Victorian lamp posts. With the Victorian Society, of which he was a co-founder in 1958, he managed to save some important buildings, including St Pancras Station. But in the 1960s two fine London buildings were demolished in spite of his campaigns: the Euston Arch and the City Coal Exchange.

In 1963 he helped fight a major conservation battle to save Bedford Park, London, the 'first garden suburb'.

The children were growing up. Paul became a jazz saxophonist and, for a time, a Mormon. Candida, one of the acclaimed beauties in her time at Oxford, married Rupert Lycett Green, whose tailor's shop, Blades, was setting men's fashions of the Swinging Sixties.

John at the Talk of the Town with his daughter Candida and her husband (left).

John himself was becoming what *The Times* called 'a teddy bear to the nation': a lovable, avuncular, crumpled figure whom millions welcomed into their homes through the television screen.

Over the years, he has been an irresistible subject for the caricaturists.

Julia Whatley

COLE 77

Burns and Betjeman...both knew the secret

Suburbia, Suburbia of thee he sings

JOHN BETJEMAN . . . specially drawn for Mirrorscope by LESLIE GIBBARD

Illingworth

Marc

Penelope had become a Roman Catholic in 1948, which was a blow to John, a staunch Church of England man. They gradually spent more time apart, but they remained on very cordial terms.

John had a 'crush' on his secretary (below), whom he called 'Freckly Jill'. He continued to draw caricatures of Penelope, as he had done since the early days of their marriage, with the characteristic down-turned mouth and hectic spots of colour in the cheeks; and to correspond with her in mock-Irish dialect.

Penelope was resuming her pre-marriage ambitions of being an Indologist. As 'Penelope Chetwode', she wrote on Indian temples, travelling over the sub-continent in far less state than when her father was Commander-in-Chief of the British Forces there.

43, CLOTH FAIR,
LONDON, E.C.1.

TREEN
TREB
WADE
CORN

19. 5. 68

Moi darlin Plymmi
'Oi can imagine the feverish sorting through & re-arranging of slides & the careful notes in yer distinctive 'andwroitin fer yer lectur on Chewzday. Oi will think of yew that day & wish Oi were there. Oi ardently be in Plymouth (of all places) so early on Wed that oi really could not coam oop. Nooni nooni. Ere yew are with Wendy in the chair.

ARS LONGA

Letter to Penelope with drawing of her lecturing on Indian temple architecture

Boot oi suppose it as its value. It makes oi realise ow mooch we lovi each other

Oi am sittin in moi little owse wroitin & wishin, oi trust, asleep upstairs. Oi am

Barry Humphries

AND DON'T PICK YOUR NOSE.

John, too, in spite of his remark to Edward James – 'Isn't abroad awful!' – was travelling more. In 1957 he had taught for a while as a visiting professor in the University of Cincinnati, USA. In the 1960s he made his first trip to Australia, where he later made a television series. What he liked most about Australia was that the Victorian architecture, being regarded as ancient, was better preserved. Through his interest in 'Aussie' he made friends with Barry Humphries, alias Dame Edna Everage and Sir Les Patterson.

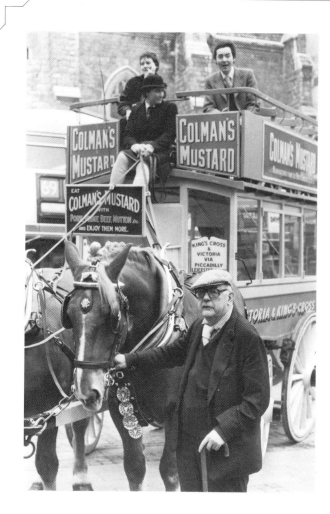

In March 1979 John travelled to the Guildhall in a horse-drawn bus, to celebrate the 105th anniversary of the London bus. Transport – especially old-style transport – was an abiding interest.

'The Battle of Bedford Park' (see page 135)

At the Memorial Service for Cecil Day Lewis, with Tamasin Day Lewis and Jill Day Lewis (Jill Balcon)

When John Masefield died in 1967, some people thought John might be chosen as the next Poet Laureate. But the post went to Cecil Day Lewis. When Day Lewis died in 1972, John was appointed to the honour which had once been Wordsworth's and Tennyson's. In 1969 he had received a knighthood.

The new Poet Laureate

He had always found it hard to write to order, and, because of his respect for the Royal Family with its special relation to the Church of England, he could not direct at them the gentle satire which enlivened so many of his poems on other subjects. His poem on Princess Anne's wedding, in 1973, provoked some dissatisfaction.

LORD CHAMBERLAIN'S OFFICE.

These are to Certify that Sir John Betjeman C.B.E. C.Litt. is by The Queen's Command, hereby appointed unto the Place and Quality of Poet Laureate in Ordinary to Her Majesty

To have, hold, exercise and enjoy the said Place together with all Rights, Profits, Privileges and Advantages thereunto belonging.

This Appointment to be during Her Majesty's Pleasure and to become void on the death of the Sovereign.

Given under my Hand and Seal this Tenth day of October 1972 in the 21st Year of Her Majesty's Reign

Maclean

LONDON 28 August-3 September 1976 Price 11p
BBC Radio London: page 54

RadioTimes

AUGUST HOLIDAY ISSUE

Betjeman's boyhood

On the day after his 70th birthday, the Poet Laureate relives his early years in a television presentation of his verse autobiography Summoned by Bells, Sunday BBC1. Back feature: Sir John remembers times past.

CHURCHILL LETTER KENNY COUNTY DONEGAL

Adrian George's drawing on a *Radio Times* cover of 1976, to mark John's 70th birthday, shows him holding *Tiger Tim's Weekly*

Osbert Lancaster thought he looked, in his battered felt hat, like an elderly Sapphic headmistress, and redrew him with silvery curls holding Radclyffe Hall's 1928 novel *The Well of Loneliness*

In 1979 John stayed at Letterkenny, Co. Donegal, to have his portrait painted by Derek Hill (frontispiece). The artist kept him entertained with gramophone records of Douglas Byng and with reminiscences of Marlborough, where he had been a pupil after John. There were visits to Lionel Perry (right), who lived nearby, and to the American Henry McIlhenny at Glenveagh Castle with its famous landscape gardens. The portrait, which was commissioned by his publisher John Murray, now hangs on Murray's staircase at 50 Albemarle Street, London.

Left to right: John G. Murray, Osbert Lancaster, Derek Hill, John Betjeman

WILLESDEN CHURCH, MIDDLESEX.

High and Low, a new collection of Betjeman poems published by Murray in 1966, included 'In Willesden Churchyard'. Charles Reade, author of *The Cloister and the Hearth*, was buried there with his friend Laura Seymour. Like John, he had once lived in New Buildings, Magdalen College, Oxford – he was a Fellow of the college – and, as John records in *An Oxford University Chest* (1938) he covered the walls in mirror glass.

Come walk with me, my love, to Neasden Lane.
The chemicals from various factories
Have bitten deep into the Portland stone
And streaked the white Carrara of the graves
Of many a Pooter and his Caroline . . .
And this, my love, is Laura Seymour's grave –
'So long the loyal counsellor and friend'
Of that Charles Reade whose coffin lies with hers.
Was she his mistress? Did he visit her
When coming down from Oxford by the coach?

In Willesden Churchyard

Homosexuality was a subject increasingly opened to public debate in the 1960s, and in *High and Low* John published two poems which touched on the subject, 'Monody on the Death of a Platonist Bank Clerk' (written in 1940) and 'Narcissus', which had first appeared in the *London Magazine*. 'Narcissus' is about a delicate, mother-dominated child. 'The Artist's Family' (below) by Thomas Matthews Rooke (1842–1942) was painted about 75 years before John's poem was written, but seems a perfect illustration of the first stanza – the Rookes' home, like that of 'Narcissus', was in Bedford Park, west London, and it too had De Morgan lustre-ware tiles round the hearth.

Yes, it was Bedford Park the vision came from –
de Morgan lustre glowing round the hearth,
And that sweet flower which self-love
                              takes its name from
Nodding among the lilies in the garth,
And Arnold Dolmetsch touching the spinet,
And Mother, Chiswick's earliest suffragette.

Narcissus

Peter Fleetwood-Hesketh had drawn the long fold-out illustration to John's book *Ghastly Good Taste* (1933) – extended to nine feet in length in the reissue of the book in 1970. In 1971 John stayed with him at the Manor House, Hale, near Liverpool, when receiving an honorary doctorate at Liverpool University. As a thank-you, he composed a poem about the house, which was published in *A Nip in the Air* (1974).

In early twilight I can hear
*   A faintly-ticking clock,*
While near and far and far and near
*   Is Liverpool baroque.*

THE MANOR HOUSE, HALE, NEAR LIVERPOOL

A Nip in the Air ('not about a Japanese aviator,' John quipped to Richard Ingrams, the editor of *Private Eye*) also contained John's seventieth birthday tribute to Lord Kinross who, as Patrick Balfour, had put John up in his house in Yeoman's Row ('the Yeo'), London, in the late 1920s. Kinross died in 1976, and John gave the address at his funeral.

How glad I am that I was bound apprentice
To Patrick's London of the 1920s.
Estranged from parents (as we all were then),
Let into Oxford and let out again,
Kind fortune led me, how I do not know,
To that Venetian flat-cum-studio
Where Patrick wrought his craft in Yeoman's Row.

FOR PATRICK, AETAT: LXX

Lord Kinross

151

Dear Mary,
        Yes, it will be bliss
To go with you by train to Diss,
Your walking shoes upon your feet;
We'll meet, my sweet, at Liverpool Street.
That levellers we may be reckoned
Perhaps we'd better travel second;
Or, lest reporters on us burst,
Perhaps we'd better travel first. . . .

A MIND'S JOURNEY TO DISS

Dial clock by William Gostling of Diss, Norfolk, *c.* 1785

Lord Drogheda has described in his autobiography, *Double Harness* (1978), how he introduced John to Mary Wilson, wife of the Prime Minister, at the première of Visconti's *Trovatore* in 1964. 'As company for her I thought that it would be a good idea to invite John Betjeman, and I said to him, "Please come and exercise your charm on the wife of the Prime Minister. Covent Garden's grant may depend on you." He duly complied. During the music he was more hypnotized by the harpist in the orchestra than by the action on the stage: but during the intervals Mrs Wilson was captivated by him. . . .' John and Mrs Wilson became great friends, and read each other their poems. In 1973 they went by train to her birthplace, Diss in Norfolk, and both wrote poems about the journey. His was published in *A Nip in the Air*.

152

the superb
iron work electrolier & lantern
combined (1 think 6 is the total)

[sketch of lantern]

made by Bambridge Reynolds

Lot 120

120 BETJEMAN (*Sir* JOHN): Four A.Ls.S., Four T.Ls.S. and One A.Pc.S., *Farnborough, Wantage* and *London*, 18 *September* 1951 *to* 5 *February* 1964, to Canon Bernard Mortlock, concerning the protection of architecture including Holy Trinity, Sloane Street and St. Olave's Churchyard, and the formation of a Victorian section of the Society for the Preservation of Ancient Buildings, and answering invitations to various engagements, *one with a pen and ink sketch, one signed 'Seán ó betjeméan', 13 pp., mostly 8vo, excluding postcard*

Mortlock shared Betjeman's passion for architecture, having published *Famous London Churches* in 1934. The latter replies to news that flood-lighting has been introduced at Holy Trinity Church, 'there were less than a year ago, lying in the porch, the superb ironwork electroliers & lanterns combined . . . they were part of a decorative scheme & went with the work of Burne Jones, Harry Wilson, Armsted, Balis, Pomeroy, Hamo Thornycroft & William Morris all of whom did work for this cathedral of the Arts and Crafts Movement', adding a sketch of the described lantern [25 *November* 1951]. When asked by the Canon to sign a petition on a Church matter he writes, 'I always feel a dreadful hypocrite when writing about Christianity, as my faith is weak and my morals are worse.' [19 *January* 1955] and in a typically Betjemanesque sentence he refuses another invitation, 'I have to give away prizes to some jolly schoolgirls in Oxford that afternoon' [25 *November* 1951]

53

Like Evelyn Waugh before him, John had made a swift transition from *enfant terrible* to Grand Old Man of English Letters. His own letters now commanded high prices at Sotheby's.

He was invited to present the prizes at Giggleswick School. His notes for his speech (left) begin with a compliment to boys and parents – 'How good looking and well dressed you all are!' – and end with the traditional request for a special holiday next term. In the speech, John described himself as 'a fraud who has got away with it.'

He was still prone to collapse with laughter or to write a spoof message on a photo of his meeting with the sex goddess Diana Dors.

153

Penelope had bought a house at Cusop, near Hay-on-Wye, surrounded by good riding country. John came to stay and enjoyed visiting 'the biggest second-hand bookshop in the world' in Hay, run by Richard Booth, the self-styled 'King of Hay'.

He publicly expressed his enthusiasm for the demotic television serial *Coronation Street*. His description of it – 'Paradise' – was used in newspaper advertisements for the north-country soap opera, and this photograph, with Jean Alexander and Bernard Youens (Hilda and Stan Ogden), was taken by the *Daily Express*.

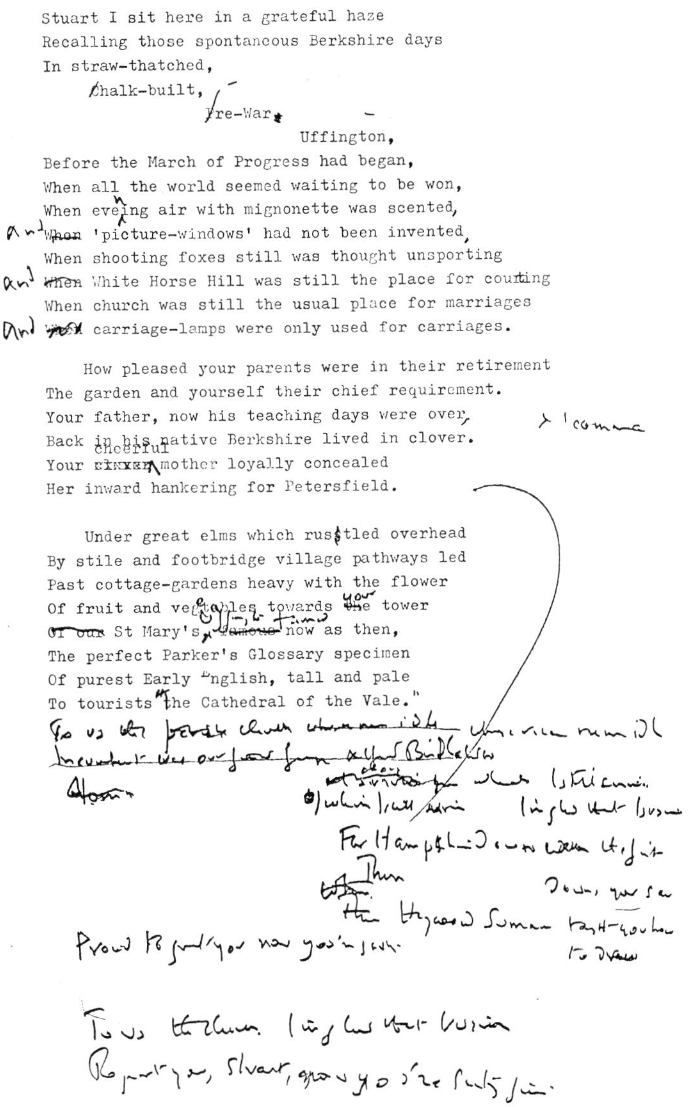

Stuart I sit here in a grateful haze
Recalling those spontaneous Berkshire days
In straw-thatched,
    chalk-built,
        pre-War
                Uffington,
Before the March of Progress had began,
When all the world seemed waiting to be won,
When eveing air with mignonette was scented,
And 'picture-windows' had not been invented,
When shooting foxes still was thought unsporting
And White Horse Hill was still the place for courting
When church was still the usual place for marriages
And carriage-lamps were only used for carriages.

   How pleased your parents were in their retirement
The garden and yourself their chief requirement.
Your father, now his teaching days were over,
Back in his native Berkshire lived in clover.
Your cheerful mother loyally concealed
Her inward hankering for Petersfield.

   Under great elms which rustled overhead
By stile and footbridge village pathways led
Past cottage-gardens heavy with the flower
Of fruit and vegetables towards your tower
Of our St Mary's, famous now as then,
The perfect Parker's Glossary specimen
Of purest Early English, tall and pale
To tourists "the Cathedral of the Vale."

STUART, I sit here in a grateful haze
Recalling those spontaneous Berkshire days
In straw-thatched,

            chalk-built,

                    pre-War

                        Uffington

Before the March of Progress had begun,
When all the world seemed waiting to be won,
When evening air with mignonette was scented,
And 'picture-windows' had not been invented,
When shooting foxes still was thought unsporting,
And White Horse Hill was still the place for courting,
When church was still the usual place for marriages
And carriage-lamps were only used for carriages.

   How pleased your parents were in their retirement
The garden and yourself their chief requirement.
Your father, now his teaching days were over,
Back in his native Berkshire lived in clover.
Your cheerful mother loyally concealed
Her inward hankering for Petersfield.
For Hampshire Downs were the first Downs you saw
And Heywood Sumner taught you there to draw.

   Under great elms which rustled overhead
By stile and foot-bridge village pathways led
To cottage gardens heavy with the flower
Of fruit and vegetables towards your tower
St Mary, Uffington, famed now as then
The perfect Parker's Glossary specimen
Of purest Early English, tall and pale,
—To tourists Cathedral of the Vale
To us the church. I'm glad that I survive
To greet you, Stuart, now you're sixty-five.

JOHN BETJEMAN

From the middle 1970s, John suffered increasingly from the onset of Parkinson's Disease. He also had a number of strokes. He wrote poems seldom now, but was induced to compose an introductory poem for a *festschrift* to his old friend Stuart Piggott, the archaeologist, who had been a neighbour in Uffington before the war. The illustration shows the final draft of the poem which preceded its eventual publication in *To illustrate the monuments: Essays on archaeology presented to Stuart Piggott*, edited by J.V.S. Megaw, Thames & Hudson, 1976.

Park Avenue to catch Betjemania

I'M NOT sure how Miss Joan Hunter-Dunn and the pine-skirted drives of Godalming will go down in New York, but I suspect that Betjeman poetry, unlike wine, will travel well.

It is certainly being given every opportunity. In mid-September the City of London Festival production of Betjemania, the musical entertainment based on Sir John's works, is being transported from All Hallows-by-the-Tower across the Atlantic to the community theatre at All Hallows' sister church, the fashionable St Bartholemew's on Park Avenue where it will be given a star-studded reception.

Canon Peter Delaney of All Hallows tells me it will be the first time that works of the Poet Laureate are to be professionally performed in the United States. Certainly the four-strong London cast including Gay Soper, who are going over there, can be sure of a glittering welcome.

Liza Minnelli is even now drumming up support for the three week event and British ambassador Sir Nicko Henderson is promised for opening night at the glamorous St Bart's, which owns its own TV studios and can boast the UN as one of its parishioners.

Whether New Yorkers go overboard for Betjeman or not, I see this as an ideal opportunity for them to become as acquainted with Stow-on-the-Wold and Leamington Spa as we are with Broadway and Cincinnati.

The *Evening Standard* had welcome news about John to relate in July 1980: *Betjemania*, the revue based on his poems, was being transferred to New York. Lisa Minnelli was reported to be 'drumming up support' for the show.

In 1971 John had moved from Cloth Fair to Radnor Walk, Chelsea, partly because of the noise caused by lorries in the early morning. At that time an antiquarian bookseller friend sold many of his papers to the University of Victoria, British Columbia, Canada. In 1980 a cache of unpublished poems by John was found in the Victoria University Library, and a selection was made by him for publication as *Uncollected Poems* (1982). It included 'St Mary Madgalen, Old Fish Street Hill':

On winter evenings I walk alone in the City
*   When cobbles glisten with wet and it's foggy and*
*   still;*
I am Rector's warden here. But more's the pity
*   We haven't the Charity children now to fill*
Our old west gallery front. Some new committee
*   Has done away with them all. I beg your pardon,*
*   I omitted to tell you where I am Rector's warden –*
At St Mary Magdalen's church, Old Fish Street Hill.

FISH STREET HILL.

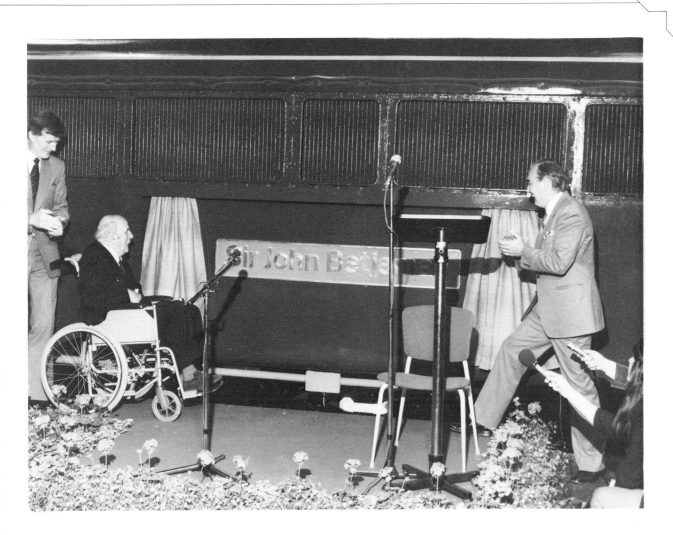

John's last public appearance was made on Friday 24 June 1983, when he named British Rail's main line locomotive number 86229 after himself at St Pancras station. Sir Peter Parker, chairman of British Rail, introducing him, said 'Sir John Betjeman is a man with an infinite capacity for taking trains'. After the naming ceremony, the 'Sir John Betjeman' hauled 'The Betjeman Pullman' from St Pancras to Bedford and back. The special train attracted a lot of attention from railway enthusiasts all along the route, as it was expected to be the only occasion when this type of locomotive, which normally operates between Euston, Birmingham, Liverpool, Manchester and Glasgow, would run on the line out of St Pancras.

The Betjeman Pullman

A unique opportunity to travel in Pullman style on the Midland Line

St Pancras - Bedford - St Pancras

on
Friday 24 June

Hauled by the newly named electric locomotive

Sir John Betjeman

Tickets on sale at St Pancras Travel Centre

£10

The naming of the locomotive Sir John Betjeman will take place at St Pancras Station on Friday 24 June starting at 1200 hours. Holders of tickets for The Betjeman Pullman will be admitted to the naming ceremony without further charge.

John Betjeman died at Trebetherick on 19 May 1984.
He had come to regard the Cornish village as 'home'.
Twelve years earlier, when he was made Poet
Laureate, Jane Bown had photographed him on the
beach there, convulsed with laughter.

> *I made hay while the sun shone.*
> *   My work sold.*
> *Now if the harvest is over*
> *   And the world cold*
> *Give me the bonus of laughter*
> *   As I lose hold.*

THE LAST LAUGH

Acknowledgements

Appreciation and thanks are due to the following for the use of illustrations. The author and the publishers have made every effort to identify copyright holders and to obtain their permission but would be glad to hear of any inadvertent errors or omissions.

Key: A above; B below; L left; R right; C centre

half title	*Express Newspapers* (photo: Sydney O'Meara)
frontis	Derek Hill Esq. and John Murray Ltd
page 8A	The late Sir John Betjeman
8B	David Herbert
9, 10L	The late Sir John Betjeman
10R, 11L	Bevis Hillier
11R	The Rector, St Cadwaladr's Church, Llangadwaladr, Anglesey
12, 13B	The late Sir John Betjeman
13A, 14	George Jones Esq.
15L	The late Sir John Betjeman
15R	Miss Mary Bouman
16A	London Borough of Camden
16R, 17AR & B	The late Sir John Betjeman
17AL & AC	Miss Mary Bouman
18AL	The late Sir John Betjeman
18AR	Phillida Gili and John Murray Ltd
18–19C	The late Sir John Betjeman
19A & B	Miss Winifred Macdonald
20A & B	The Hon. Lady Betjeman
20L	BBC Hulton Picture Library
21	The Tate Gallery, London
22A	Marshall, Keene & Co., Hove
22B, 23	The late Sir John Betjeman
24–5	The Headmaster, Dragon School, Oxford
26	Bevis Hillier
27A	The Rector, St Ervan's Church, Cornwall
27B	The Rector, St Endellion's Church, Cornwall
28A	Bevis Hillier
28B	Duncan Andrews Collection
29A	Mrs Joan Kunzer
29B, 30	Bevis Hillier
31A	Michael Strout
31B	Bevis Hillier
32A	Valentines of Dundee Ltd
32B	Lodenek Press Ltd, Padstow
33A	Bevis Hillier
33B	Mr and Mrs Dearden
34	Mrs Kenneth Crookshank
35, 36A	The late Sir John Betjeman
36BL	Lady Elton
36BR	Wilfred Blunt Esq.
37A	Bevis Hillier
37B	BBC Hulton Picture Library
37C	The Master, Marlborough College
38–40	Bevis Hillier
41L	The late Sir John Betjeman
41R, 42B	Professor John Bowle
42A	*Country Life* (IPC Magazines Ltd)
43L	The Master, Marlborough College
43R	Bevis Hillier
44AL & BL	The late Sir John Betjeman
44R	Clive Aslet Esq.
45L	University of Victoria Library
45AR	The late Sir John Betjeman
45BR, 46	Bevis Hillier
47A	Camera Press Ltd
47B, 48L	The Editor, *Isis*, Oxford
48R	University of Victoria Library
49AL & BL	Mrs J.M. Thompson
49R	Oxford & County Newspapers
50A & B	The Earl and Countess of Longford
51L	BBC Hulton Picture Library
51AR	Frances, Lady Fergusson of Kilkerran (photo: Michael Dugdale)
51BR	Sir Osbert Lancaster. © John Murray Ltd
52L	Martyn Skinner Esq.
52R	Eric Walter White Esq.
53	Frances, Lady Fergusson of Kilkerran
54AL	The late Sir John Betjeman
54AR	The Hon. Lady Betjeman
54B, 55B	Frances, Lady Fergusson of Kilkerran (photo: Michael Dugdale)
55A	David Synnott Esq.
56	The Editor, *Isis*, Oxford
57	Lady Harrod
58L	Duncan Andrews Collection
58R	The Editor, *Isis*, Oxford
59 *far* L	Bevis Hillier
59 L & R, 60	The Editor, *Isis*, Oxford
61L	Edouard Roditi Esq.
61AR	Frances, Lady Fergusson of Kilkerran (photo: Michael Dugdale)
61BR	Edward James Esq.
62A	The Leger Galleries Ltd
62BR	Lady Harrod
63AL	Bevis Hillier
63AR	The Editor, *Isis*, Oxford
63BR	The Editor, *Isis*, © in poem John Murray Ltd
64L	© Herbert Jenkins 1928
64R	The Editor, *Isis*, Oxford
65	A.G. Swift Esq.
66–7	David Synnott Esq.
68	*Oxford and Cambridge Magazine* (photos: Derrick Witty)
69	The Editor, *Isis*, Oxford
70	David Soltau Esq.
71AL	G.R. Barkley Smith Esq.
71AR	Kenric Rice Esq.
71BR	The Plunkett Foundation, Oxford
72A	Alan Nightingale Esq.
72B	David Soltau Esq.
73A	Alan Nightingale Esq.
73B	Duncan Andrews Collection
74L	Mrs Walter Moule and *Middlesex County Times*
74R	Mrs Walter Moule
75	Mrs M. Geddes
76L	The late Sir John Betjeman
76R, 77	Christopher Sykes Esq.
78–9	The Earl and Countess of Longford
80AL	Lady Harrod
80BL	*Oxford and Cambridge Magazine* (photo: Derrick Witty)
80AR & BR, 81–3, 84A	The Hon. Thomas Pakenham
84B	The late Sir John Betjeman
85L	Bevis Hillier
85R	Frances, Lady Fergusson of Kilkerran
86L & C	The late Sir John Betjeman
86AR	The Architectural Press Ltd
86B, 87A	The Hon. Mrs Derek Jackson
87B	Duncan Andrews Collection
88–9	The Hon. Mrs Derek Jackson
90–91, 92BL & R	The Hon. Lady Betjeman
92AL	The Hon. Mrs Derek Jackson
93	The Hon. Lady Betjeman
94A	Lady Harrod
94B	The late Sir John Betjeman
95A	Sir Osbert and Lady Lancaster
95B	Blackie & Son Ltd
96A	Bevis Hillier
96B	Peter Fleetwood-Hesketh Esq. and Chapman & Hall Ltd
97L	Chapman & Hall Ltd
97R	The Hon. Mrs Derek Jackson
98	David Herbert
99	The Hon. Lady Betjeman
100AL	Express Newspapers
100BL & R	Duncan Andrews Collection
101A	Frances, Lady Fergusson of Kilkerran (photo: Michael Dugdale)
101BL	Lady Harrod
101BR	The Hon. Lady Betjeman
102L	Lady Harrod
102AR	Sir Osbert Lancaster
102BR	The Lady Mary Clive
103–5	The Hon. Lady Betjeman
106	Robert Heber-Percy Esq.
107A	The Hon. Lady Betjeman
107C & B	Frances, Lady Fergusson of Kilkerran (photo: Michael Dugdale)
108	The Hon. Lady Betjeman
109L	A Shell photograph
109C	Private Collection. © Laurence Whistler Esq.
109AR	William Scudamore Mitchell Esq.
109B	Shell UK Ltd
110L	William Scudamore Mitchell Esq.

110A John Murray Ltd
110BR Illustrated London News Picture Library
111–12, 113A The Hon. Lady Betjeman
113B BBC copyright photograph
114L The Hon. Lady Betjeman
114AR BBC Hulton Picture Library
114BR Bevis Hillier
115 Duncan Andrews Collection
116AR The Hon. Lady Betjeman
116BL Bevis Hillier
116BR Mrs Ion Villiers-Stuart (photo: Jimmy Walshe)
117 The Hon. Lady Betjeman
118L *Irish Times*
118AR Bevis Hillier
118BR University of Victoria Library
119L Mrs Harold Wycliffe Jackson
119AR Bevis Hillier
119BR BBC copyright photograph
120A Bassano Studios and The Hon. Lady Betjeman
120B The late Sir John Betjeman
121A The Hon. Lady Betjeman
121B © Sir Osbert Lancaster and John Murray Ltd
121C The late Sir John Betjeman
122AL The Hon. Lady Betjeman
122BL New York Public Library (Astor, Lennox & Tilden Foundation)
122R Express Newspapers
123A & L The late Sir John Betjeman
123BR The Café Royal
124AL Duncan Andrews Collection
124BL The late Sir John Betjeman
124–5C Fox Photos Ltd
125A Sotheby Parke Bernet & Co.
125R BBC Hulton Picture Library

126L The Hon. Lady Betjeman
126A photo Mark Kauffman. © Life Magazine
126BR photo Douglas Glass
127, 128L The Hon. Lady Betjeman
128R, 129AL Bevis Hillier
129AR & B The Hon. Lady Betjeman
130 Mr and Mrs John Piper
131A The Hon. Thomas Pakenham
131B The Hon. Lady Betjeman
132A Lady Harrod
132B John Hadfield and *The Saturday Book 16*
133L Sir Osbert Lancaster
133R photo: David Farrell
134AL *The Times*
134A & B Express Newspapers
135L The Hon. Lady Betjeman
135AR & B GLC Historic Buildings Division
136, 137AR The Hon. Lady Betjeman
137L photo: Mark Kauffman. © Life Magazine
137BR Mark Gerson
138, 139AL photo: David Farrell
139AR photo: Bill Worsfold
139B *The Observer* (photo: David Sim)
140A Julia Whatley
140AR Cole
140B Express Newspapers
141A © Mirror Group Newspapers
141BL *Daily Mail*
141BR Mark Boxer Esq.
142A & B The Hon. Lady Betjeman
142L The late Sir John Betjeman
143AL & AR The Hon. Lady Betjeman
143BL Duncan Andrews Collection
143BR photo: John Timbers
144AL *The Guardian*

144R *The Observer* (photo: David Sim)
145 Duncan Andrews Collection
146L Keystone Press Agency
146R The late Sir John Betjeman
147L The Lord Chamberlain's Office
147R Express Newspapers
148L *Radio Times*
148AR Derek Hill Esq.
148BR Sir Osbert Lancaster
149A The late Lionel Perry Esq.
149B The late Sir John Betjeman
150L Bevis Hillier
150R Jeremy Cooper Esq.
151A Peter Fleetwood-Hesketh Esq.
151B Lady Harrod
152L BBC Hulton Picture Library
152C & B Bevis Hillier
153L Sotheby & Co.
153AR photo: John Garret
153BR The late Sir John Betjeman
154A The Hon. Lady Betjeman
154B Express Newspapers
155L The late Sir John Betjeman
155R Thames & Hudson Ltd
156L Express Newspapers
156R Bevis Hillier
157 British Rail
158 *The Observer* (photo: Jane Bown)
Jacket front photo Mark Kauffmann © Life Magazine
back BBC copyright photograph

The author would also like to thank Miss Doris Baum and Mr Alan Bell for their help, the publishers John G. Murray, David and Brenda Herbert and Ayeshah Haleem for their sympathetic editing, and Trevor Vincent for designing the book so well.